One Child, Two Languages

ONE CHILD, TWO LANGUAGES
A GUIDE FOR PRESCHOOL EDUCATORS
OF CHILDREN LEARNING ENGLISH
AS A SECOND LANGUAGE

by

Patton O. Tabors, Ed.D.
Graduate School of Education
Harvard University
Cambridge, Massachusetts

Baltimore • London • Toronto • Sydney

Paul H. Brookes Publishing Co.
Post Office Box 10624
Baltimore, Maryland 21285-0624

Typeset by A.W. Bennett, Inc., Hartland, Vermont.
Manufactured in the United States of America by
Thomson-Shore, Inc., Dexter, Michigan.

All of the individuals in this book have been given pseudonyms to protect
their privacy.

The photograph on page vii is by Richard Tabors. All other photographs in the
book were taken by Patton.

This book is an expansion of an earlier chapter by Tabors, P., & Snow, C.E.
(1994). English as a second language in preschools. In F. Genesee (Ed.), *Educating second language children: The whole child, the whole curriculum, the whole community* (pp. 103–125). New York: Cambridge University Press. Portions of the
chapter have been reprinted throughout the book with the permission of
Cambridge University Press.

The cartoon ROSE IS ROSE by Pat Brady, which appears on page 9, is
reprinted by permission of United Features Syndicate, Inc.

The social and cognitive strategies that appear on pages 76–79 are reprinted
from Wong Fillmore, L. (1979). Individual differences in second language
acquisition. In C.J. Fillmore, D. Kempler, & W. S-Y. Wang (Eds.), *Individual differences in language ability and language behavior* (pp. 209–218). New York: Academic Press; reprinted by permission.

Library of Congress Cataloging-in-Publication Data
Tabors, Patton O.
      One child, two languages :   a guide for preschool educators of
   children learning English as a second language / by Patton O.
   Tabors.
         p.   cm.
      Includes bibliographical references (p.   ) and index.
      ISBN 1-55766-272-X
      1. English language—Study and teaching (Preschool)—Foreign
   speakers.   2. Children of immigrants—Education—United States.
   3. Language arts (Preschool)—United States.   4. Bilingualism in
   children—United States.   5. Children—Language.   I. Title.
   PE1128.A2T23   1997
   372.65'21044—DC20   96-36565
                                                                      CIP

British Library Cataloguing in Publication data are available from the British
Library.

Contents

About the Author

Patton O. Tabors, Ed.D., is Research Associate in the Projects in Language Development at the Graduate School of Education at Harvard University. For the past 9 years, Dr. Tabors has been the Research Coordinator of the Home-School Study of Language and Literacy Development,  a longitudinal study of low-income, English-speaking children and their families. For the past 4 years, she has also directed research related to the mother–child book-reading project of the Manpower Development Research Corporation's evaluations of New Chance and JOBS training programs.

   Pursuing an interest that developed while teaching bilingual students in the Cambridge Public Schools, Dr. Tabors entered the doctoral program at the Graduate School of Education at Harvard University in 1981 to study first- and second-language acquisition. Her qualifying paper and dissertation research, based on 2 years of ethnographic investigation in a nursery school classroom, resulted in the delineation of the developmental pathway for young children learning English as a second language. In 1989, she used this information in planning a trilingual preschool/primary school for the University of Massachusetts, Lowell. In 1995, Dr. Tabors became coordinator of the Harvard Language Diversity Project, a research activity of the New England Quality Research Center on Head Start.

While writing *One Child, Two Languages,* Dr. Tabors was able to visit preschool classrooms, interview teachers, and hold workshops related to the topic of young children learning English as a second language. Recognizing the importance of a continuing dialogue on this topic, she has established an e-mail account (patton@onechild.com) and a World Wide Web site (http://www.onechild.com) so that teachers, administrators, and any other interested individuals can respond to the information in the book.

Foreword

Every June *The Boston Globe* publishes a picture and brief biography of each of the valedictorians from Boston-area high schools. This year, like all those in the recent past, the vast majority of the valedictorians whose pictures were published—the students selected as the best in their schools—were immigrants to the United States. They had come here with their parents as 3-year-olds or 6-year-olds or perhaps even as 10- or 12-year-olds. These are not the immigrants we hear described by some politicians, immigrants who are exploiting American generosity or threatening the American way of life. These are immigrants whose parents have sacrificed to give their children a better chance, who have chosen educational achievement as their route to success, who have embraced the American dream, who have worked hard at their studies and often at after-school jobs as well, and who will be the doctors and scientists and engineers we need for the approaching 21st century. These valedictorians, and their many successful immigrant classmates, managed to learn English at some point on their path to academic accomplishment.

For immigrant children who arrive in the United States old enough to attend elementary school, a variety of programs exist to receive them and to help them adjust to a new culture and a new language. Since the mid-1960s, educators have had experience with bilingual education and with teaching English as a second language to school-age children; consequently, there is now a solid body of practical experience and research evidence available to inform good practice.

Immigrant children who arrive before the age of 6 have, until now, been largely ignored. One of the most widespread and harmful myths in our society is that very young children will

best, most amount

learn a second language automatically, quickly, and easily—with no special attention to their needs for an optimal learning environment. Thus, as a society we have hardly considered ways to help these preschool children learn English; nor have we thought much about how to help them maintain their home language. The preschool and Head Start teachers whose classes are increasingly populated by non–English-speaking children have been constructing their responses to these new challenges with little help and sometimes with considerable puzzlement.

One Child, Two Languages is designed to inform, stimulate, and help anyone serving young second-language learners. It draws on observations of classrooms where such children are learning English, on interviews with experienced teachers of English-learning children, and on research about second-language acquisition and bilingualism. By describing a variety of children learning English in different classroom settings, it invites preschool classroom teachers to be reflective about the impact of their curricula, their classroom organization, and their assessment practices on non–English-speaking children. This book offers practical tools such as suggestions for interviews with parents and for appropriate assessments of young children, but, more important, it makes accessible the information that reflective practitioners need in order to improve their own practice.

In this book the author defines the double-bind that second-language learners face; that is, they cannot learn the new language unless they can engage in social interaction with those who speak the new language, but they have limited social access to those individuals until they learn the new language. This society faces a similar double-bind—one in which fear of the different prevents the contact that would dissolve the fear. We are unable to benefit from the rich cultural and linguistic diversity of this nation as long as we view the immigrants who bring that diversity as threatening and troublesome. We cannot get to know what we fear, and we cannot reduce the fear without knowledge. Suzette Haden Elgin, a linguist and novelist, described in her trilogy *Native Tongue* (Elgin, S.H. [1994]. Bergenfield, NJ: New American Library/New York: Daw Books) a future world in which communication between Terrans and the many races of aliens in contact with the planet Terra is made possible by the existence of a caste of Linguists—specialists in the alien languages. Linguist children in Elgin's world learn the alien languages by spending several hours a day in specially designed interfaces, together with alien young, for the first several years of their lives. These children subsequently grow up to assume positions of great power and responsibility, which they obtain because of their capacities as translators and interpreters. We might think of North American preschools as low-tech interfaces where children sharing experiences at the water table, during circle time, and as they have snack come to enjoy mutual understanding and effective communication across linguistic boundaries. In the best preschool classrooms, this is happening right now. In others, it may take only minor adjustments to ensure optimal communication and optimal language learning. Such adjustments may be our best hope of devising our own effective interfaces, thus creating a society (in the next generation, if not this one) that embraces diversity and celebrates multilingualism as well as one in which all children have access to the power and benefits derived from speaking English well.

Catherine E. Snow, Ph.D.
Henry Lee Shattuck Professor of Education
Graduate School of Education
Harvard University
Cambridge, Massachusetts

Preface

The title of this book *One Child, Two Languages: A Guide for Preschool Educators of Children Learning English as a Second Language* reflects its dual focus on children as language learners and teachers as facilitators of children's language learning. In fact, the book is divided into two parts. The first part details the second-language–learning child's task and the second part discusses the role that the teacher can play in helping children during the second-language–learning process.

Furthermore, the title is meant to convey that young children can and do learn two (or more) languages, and that this process involves adding a second language to a first language rather than replacing a first language with a second. For the purposes of this book, the language being discussed as the second language is English. The information presented in this book about learning English as a second language, however, would be the same no matter what second language an individual child was learning. Although the second-language–learning process is the topic of the book, this is not meant to imply that a child's home-language development should not also be supported and developed. For this reason, strategies that can help educators and parents continue to support first-language acquisition are included in the book as well.

This book is written primarily for preschool educators, as the children who were involved in the research presented here were, for the most part, 3–5 years old. However, the developmental sequence of second-language learning and the techniques for support and facilitation of the second-language–learning process that are discussed in the book are also applicable throughout the early childhood period. The recommendations in this book, on the whole, therefore, can be implemented within the context of any developmental classroom, making it possible for early childhood educators to take advantage of them without major organizational or curricular changes.

Planning preschool programs for second-language–learning children will require additional information beyond what preschool educators already know about child development. Information about the importance of the cultural and linguistic backgrounds of second-language–learning children, the course that second-language learning is likely to take in preschool-age children, the supportive techniques that teachers can use in their classrooms, and the part that second-language learners' families' plans may play in linguistic and educational decisions will need to be integrated into their basic knowledge of child development. The main goal of this book is to provide this information so that preschool teachers and administrators can develop effective programs for young second-language learners in the context of planning for all children.

Acknowledgments

I wish to thank the colleagues who have discussed the material in this book with me, the preschool administrators who have given me access to their programs, the teachers whose classrooms I have visited and whose wisdom I have tapped in workshops and interviews, and the children who have accepted me into their world and let me eavesdrop on their very important conversations.

ONE CHILD, TWO LANGUAGES

chapter one

Introduction

Three-year-old Chantal lives in a small city in Massachusetts with her 5-year-old brother, her 20-year-old half-sister, and her mother and father. Chantal and her brother were born in Massachusetts, but their parents and their half-sister are originally from Haiti, having immigrated in the early 1990s during a time of political strife. Chantal's father works at a hospital as an orderly, and her half-sister takes English as a Second Language classes at the community college and has a job as a housekeeper at a local hotel. Chantal speaks Kreyol at home with her family.

This year Chantal has been enrolled in a Head Start classroom near her home. When she first came to the Head Start classroom, she did not speak any English, but, over the course of the year, she has begun to use some English during interactions with the English-speaking teachers and children. When Chantal's mother comes to pick her up each day, she nods and smiles at the teachers, but is unable to carry on any conversation with them about Chantal's activities. After helping to clear one of the tables used for the children's lunch, Chantal's mother collects Chantal and leaves the classroom. When the teachers want to schedule a home visit with Chantal's mother, they ask the social services

worker who speaks Kreyol to make the appointment and to come on the visit to translate for them.

Chantal's family is just one of the many families that have immigrated to the United States in the last decades of the 20th century. The U.S. Census Bureau reports that in 1994 nearly 32 million (or 1 in 7) people in the United States spoke a language other than English at home (Headden, 1995). It is estimated that 2.6 million children attending public school in the same year came from homes in which English was not the first language, an increase of 76% over the previous decade (Hornblower, 1995).

Not surprisingly, the arrival of large numbers of immigrant families has had an effect on preschool education as well. For example, Head Start classrooms, like the one attended by Chantal, have experienced a sharp increase in the number of children enrolled from other than English-speaking homes. In 1994, a bilingual/multicultural survey sponsored by the Administration for Children, Youth and Families (SocioTechnical Research Applications, Inc., 1996) found that 91% of the responding Head Start programs reported an increase in at least one cultural or linguistic group during the preceding 5 years. The survey, which received responses from 69% of the 2,006 Head Start programs queried, reports that 128,780 of the children surveyed (23.9%)

were reported to have a first language other than English. Although 74% of the children spoke English at home, 22% spoke Spanish, and the remaining 4% came from families whose members spoke any one of the other 139 languages represented among the children in the survey.

Although nearly one third of the programs reported that only one home language was spoken by the children in their classrooms, another third of the programs reported having children from two different first-language backgrounds, and the remaining one third reported 3 to as many as 10 home languages spoken by the children in their programs (SocioTechnical Research Applications, Inc., 1996). These effects are not equally distributed throughout the United States: The highest percentage of children who are reported to be limited in English proficiency (55%) are in Head Start programs in New York, New Jersey, Puerto Rico, and the Virgin Islands; the lowest percentage (2%) are in programs in Iowa, Kansas, Missouri, and Nebraska.

The Head Start population, of course, represents only a fraction of the young children in preschool programs in the United States. One estimate (Kagan & Garcia, 1991) is that there will be 5.2 million preschoolers from other than English-speaking homes in the United States by the year 2000. It can be anticipated that a large percentage of these preschoolers will be Spanish speaking, but that a myriad of other languages will be represented as well. Although preschool programs in certain areas of the United States will be most heavily affected, almost all preschool programs will be affected in some way. Planning ways to effectively serve these preschoolers is now a major challenge for preschool educators.

PRESCHOOL EDUCATION SETTINGS FOR CHILDREN FROM OTHER THAN ENGLISH-SPEAKING HOMES

Preschool education programs, from small family child care programs, to private or public preschool programs or child care facilities, to federally funded Head Start programs, have responded to the arrival of children from other than English-speaking homes by developing programs that respond to the linguistic needs of these children in different ways. One useful way to categorize these programs is related to how language is used in the classroom.

Preschool educational settings can be divided into three major categories related to language use (see Table 1). The first type of setting is one in which the home or first language of the child is the primary language of the classroom. For Spanish-speaking children, this means that the teachers must be native speakers of Spanish; for Arabic speakers, this means that the teachers must be native speakers of Arabic. This kind of classroom is a *first-language classroom.*

Advocates of first-language classrooms for children from other than English-speaking homes (e.g., Wong Fillmore, 1991b) emphasize the importance of the development of the first language as a necessary basis for later literacy and consequently later school success. These advocates are particularly concerned that young children are highly susceptible to losing their first language if the first language is not strongly maintained during the

Table 1.   Types of preschool education settings for children from other than English-speaking homes in the United States

	First-language classroom	Bilingual classroom	English-language classroom
Teachers	Native speakers of L1[a]	Bilingual in L1 and English *or* native speaker of L1 paired with native speaker of English	Native speakers of English
Children	Native speakers of L1	All native speakers of L1 *or* mixture of L1 and English speakers	Native speakers of L1 *or* native speakers of different L1s *or* either of above and English speakers
Classroom organization	All interaction in L1	Interaction split between L1 and English	All interaction in English
Language outcomes	Development of L1; no development of English	Maintenance or development of L1, while also developing English	Development of English; no maintenance or development of L1

[a]L1 = any specific native language that is not English.

preschool years. Their conclusion, therefore, is that children should attend first-language preschool education settings and should not be exposed to a second-language setting before elementary school. Even then, they believe, there should be a strong developmental first-language program throughout the early elementary years in order to establish literacy in the first language.

A second type of preschool education setting is one in which there are individual teachers who are themselves bilingual or there are two teachers who have different language backgrounds. For instance, in a classroom that serves Mandarin-speaking children, one teacher in the classroom may be English speaking, and the other may speak Mandarin; or in a classroom that serves children who have recently come to the United States from Haiti, the teacher may be a Kreyol-English bilingual. In these situations, language choice becomes an issue: What language is being spoken to whom by whom and under what circumstances? This type of classroom is a *bilingual classroom.*

Bilingual preschool education settings may take a variety of forms. In some settings, all of the children come from one particular other than English-language background and only the teacher or teachers provide English language input to the children. At the other end of the spectrum are two-way–bilingual programs, in which approximately half of the children in any given classroom are from the same other than English-speaking backgrounds and the other half are from English-speaking backgrounds, and instruction is evenly split between the two languages. In this situation, each child's first language is being supported, while a second language is being added, and children have second-language input from other children, not just from their teacher.

The third type of preschool education setting is one in which the primary language is English, even though there are children in the classroom whose home language is not English. In this situation, the teachers may have little or no proficiency in a language other than English, and they may have children from only one language group or from many different language groups in their classroom. This type of classroom is an *English-language classroom.*

In an English-language classroom, the teacher or teachers use English for almost all interactions; therefore, a child whose home language is not English will not have his or her language supported in this classroom, although there may be other children from the same language background with whom to talk and play. These classrooms can be a more or less welcoming location for a child whose home language is not English, depending on how multicultural the curriculum is and on what efforts the teachers make to bring parents and other cultural representatives into the classroom.

In the real world, of course, it is sometimes difficult to categorize actual programs. These categories, therefore, are meant merely as guidelines, so that teachers and administrators of preschool education settings can locate their programs in relation to a set of features that have been found to be consistent across a variety of settings.

These categories are also useful when thinking about the material in this book. Because much of the research and most of the examples in this book come from an English-language preschool education setting, it is this setting that serves as a baseline for discussing second-language learning in young children. In addition, discussions of how language acquisition processes would differ in a bilingual classroom are included. Because second-language acquisition is not a goal of first-language classrooms, they are not a topic of this book except when discussed with regard to supplementary settings, such as special purpose Saturday or Sunday schools.

FIRST- AND SECOND-LANGUAGE DEVELOPMENT

When young children like Chantal are enrolled in an English-language or bilingual preschool education setting, they begin the process of second-language acquisition. In order to start the process of thinking about second-language acquisition, it is useful first to review how children learn a first language and then use that process as a contrast to second-language learning.

First-Language Acquisition

All typically developing children learn a first language, whatever that language may be. This process, which occurs in the context of social interaction within the child's family structure, begins with the production of recognizable sounds around the age of 1 year and continues intensively throughout the preschool period. In fact, although most of the basic skills of oral language are acquired by the time a child is about 5 years old, more advanced uses of language (e.g., debating, lecturing) may continue to be acquired well into adulthood, and vocabulary acquisition is a lifelong process.

Acquiring a first language is a monumental task. In order to understand what a large task this is, one might think of the language system as a puzzle with a variety of interlocking pieces, all of which must fit together in order for the puzzle to be complete. There are five pieces to this puzzle: 1) *phonology,* or the sounds of the language; 2) *vocabulary,* or the words of the language; 3) *grammar,* or how the words are put together to make sentences in the language; 4) *discourse,* or how sentences are put together to, for example, tell stories, make an argument, or explain how something works; and 5) *pragmatics,* or the rules about how to use the language. In order for children to be considered native speakers of a language, they must have control over all of these aspects of the language system. Developing this control is a major undertaking of the first 5 years of a child's life. In the following discussion, the first-language–acquisition process is discussed using English as the example language, but the same discussion could apply to other languages just as well.

The process of language development begins with a baby's babbling. At first, babies babble a wide variety of sounds; over time, they begin to restrict their babbling to sounds they hear in words spoken by those around them. When infants being raised in an English-speaking environment are 5–8 months old, they start producing syllables like *ba, ma,* and *ga* in the course of their babbling. Open syllables like these are relatively easy to pronounce and thus form the basis for many "baby talk" words like *mama, booboo,* and *peepee.* Words that contain closed syllables, those with a consonant at the end, are harder to pronounce, especially if quite different consonants need to be articulated within one syllable. Thus, young children learning English often say "goggie" for "doggie" or "guck" for "truck," because they simply cannot yet put two such different sounds as /g/ and /d/ or /t/ into one syllable.

Between 12 and 18 months, most babies produce their first word or words, having made the connection between certain groups of sounds and objects or certain groups of sounds and "getting things done." A baby's first 50 words usually contain a mix of different types of words: names for important people like *daddy*, object names like *cookie*, functional words like *up*, and social words like *bye-bye*.

After acquiring a number of words, children begin demonstrating an understanding of the grammatical requirements of language by combining first two and then more words, developing the ability to express more complex relationships with their words. At first a child will say "kitty" to represent everything from "there's a cat" to "I'm scared of that cat," and it will be necessary for an adult to interpret the full meaning. Soon, however, the child will combine "kitty" with an attribute like "pretty," an action like "bite," or a location like "outside," thus beginning the process of building the grammatical units that are sentences.

Throughout this period, children are also learning the proper ways to use their words. In the United States *hi* and *bye-bye* are early acquired words, perhaps because parents work hard to get their babies to produce these words at the proper times to show that they are being correctly socialized. At the same time, babies also learn the turn-taking rules of conversation, often before they have anything to contribute to the conversation. In exchanges between mothers and infants, mothers even consider burps as appropriate turn-taking moves by babies.

The process of learning the culturally appropriate way to use language continues throughout the preschool years as children learn the rules of politeness and the "ins" and "outs" of what can appropriately be said where, when, under what conditions, and to whom. Because these rules are complicated and subtle, young children often violate them, giving the authors of cartoons a wealth of material.

During the preschool years children engage in extended oral language development. Building on the earlier development of sounds, children begin work on rhyming and identifying initial sounds in words, often showing endless fascination with this type of word play. At the same time, they acquire a staggering 6–10 new words a day, while also broadening their understanding of the meanings of the words they already know.

Children also begin to acquire the more complicated forms of grammar during this time period; in English these are past tenses, embedded clauses, and passive constructions. This proc-

ROSE IS ROSE ® by Pat Brady

ROSE IS ROSE reprinted by permission of United Feature Syndicate, Inc.

ess frequently results in creative mistakes like "My mom breakeded the plate," which show that children are noticing consistent patterns and applying them to the language system as they understand it.

A distinctive accomplishment of this period is the development of the ability to construct discourse. Preschool-age children begin to participate in the construction of explanations, the development of arguments, and the telling of narratives. In American culture, these efforts begin by being coconstructed with older siblings or an adult who asks appropriate questions or contributes to the discourse, followed by the child gradually taking on more of the burden of the telling until he or she can produce the type of discourse independently (see Figure 1).

During this time, children also learn to modify what they are saying depending on the audience. A child, for example, learns that he has to give Aunt Sarah, who does not know all of his friends, a lot more background information about *who, why,* and *where* before launching into a story about a disaster at the playground.

Second-Language Acquisition

Some young children not only develop language skills in a first language, but also develop them in a second language. When this happens, the child is considered to be involved in a process of second-language acquisition.

There are two types of second-language acquisition among young children: simultaneous and sequential acquisition. *Simultaneous acquisition* of two languages occurs when children are exposed to both languages from a very early age, sometimes as a result of each parent speaking a separate language with the child

Brad:	I want to go to the ice cream store.
Mother:	**Well, you can't. It's raining.**
Brad:	Did you see the ice cream store man go home?
Mother:	I don't know. I don't know what time they close. Maybe we could put on our rain coats.
Brad:	Do you got a rain coat?
Mother:	No, but I'll wear something.
Grandmother:	I'll let Mommy use my umbrella.
Brad:	If she has . . . (Thunder cracks outside). Thunder.
Mother:	Thunder.
Grandmother:	Mmhm.
Brad:	*We can run to the ice cream store. Then we can run back home. And so the thunder won't get us, right?*
Mother:	Right.
Grandmother:	**You know what the thunder is?**
Brad:	**Yeah. Thunder and lightning.**
Grandmother:	**Yeah. And the thunder is when the angels are upstairs bowling. And that's one of them just got a spare.**
Mother:	Brad should get out his Berenstain Bear. I'm going to have to let Ma read it and that'll tell her what thunder is, huh? (laughing)
Grandmother:	Mmhm.
Mother:	Tells all about thunder and . . .
Grandfather:	**That's the energy. Thunder is caused by energy in the clouds.**
Brad:	*Yeah, but one day I was sleeping in my bed for a long long time and thunder and lightning came from outside and I was trying to find something that was yellow outside in the dark all by itself. And it came out. And it was thunder and lightning and I hided from it.*
Grandfather:	*And you hided from it?*
Brad:	*Yeah.*
Grandfather:	*Where'd you hide? Under your blankets?*
Brad:	*No, under my covers. Like when I was sleeping.*
Grandfather:	Do you always pull the covers up over your head? Yeah?

Figure 1. A mealtime conversation showing explanations (distinguished in bold) and narratives (distinguished in italic) between Brad (3½ years old) and his mother, grandmother, and grandfather. (From Beals, D., & Snow, C. [1994]. "Thunder is when the angels are upstairs bowling": Narratives and explanations at the dinner table. *Journal of Narrative and Life History, 4*(4), 341–343; reprinted by permission.)

or both parents speaking one language and a caregiver speaking another language with the child. *Sequential acquisition* occurs when a child begins to learn a second language after the first language is at least partly established.

Simultaneous Acquisition   When young children are exposed to two languages from birth, there is often an initial period of acquiring words in one or the other of the languages. Children will, however, quickly demonstrate a capacity to keep their two languages separate and often display an early developing understanding of when one or the other of their languages should be used (see Fantini, 1985; Saunders, 1988; Taeschner, 1983, for case studies).

Taeschner (1983), for example, writes about raising her two daughters as German-Italian bilinguals living in Rome. Although she is a German-Italian bilingual herself, Taeschner spoke only German with her children, and her husband, a native speaker of Italian, spoke only Italian with the girls. By the time the older daughter, Lisa, was 1½ years old, she had a total of 18 words: 6 in German, 6 in Italian, and 6 that would work in either language (e.g., *mamma*). Lisa was using 100 words 5 months later: 46 were Italian, 34 were German, and 20 (many of which were names for people) would work in either language. In the intervening time period, Lisa had had more contact with Italian speakers as she had spent time with an Italian grandparent and aunt, as well as with an Italian-speaking caregiver. As Taeschner remarks,

> It is clear that there is a close relationship between the amount of contact with each language and the child's linguistic output; the quantity of contact the child had with each language determined the quantity of words she learned. When Lisa had more opportunities of speaking Italian, her output increased, and the same was true of German. (p. 194)

Although some parents and educators have worried about the possibility of language confusion in the situation in which children are exposed to two languages from birth (see Meisel, 1989, for evidence against language confusion), researchers now believe that, far from being a problem, the process of acquiring two languages from a very early age has cognitive as well as social benefits (Hakuta, 1986).

Sequential Acquisition   Other children acquire a second language after the basis for their first language has been established. This sequential acquisition of a second language occurs, for instance, when a young child like Chantal enters a preschool setting in which her home language is not the language used in the classroom. It is this type of second-language acquisition that is the topic of this book.

If a child learns two languages simultaneously, and if those two languages are developed equally during childhood, then the language development process is expected to be the same for both languages. In any sequential second-language acquisition situation, however, there are a number of factors that make the two processes different.

First, second-language learners, even very young ones, already have prior knowledge about language and its uses. In the process of learning a first language, they have determined what communication is all about, and, furthermore, what particular systems and styles of communication work in their immediate environment. For these children, then, second-language acquisition is not a process of discovering what language *is,* but rather of discovering what *this* language is.

Second, unlike first-language acquisition, which is a feature of a specific developmental period in a child's life, second-language acquisition can be undertaken at any age. There are two variables related to second-language acquisition and age: *cognitive capacity* and *cognitive demand*. The older a child is when faced with any cognitive challenge, the greater the child's cognitive capacity will be to take on that challenge. A high school student obviously has many more intellectual skills to bring to bear in any learning situation than does a student in kindergarten. The cognitive demands of the tasks that a high school student faces, however, are also much greater than those faced by a student in kindergarten. The idea that young children are facile, even magically rapid, language learners is no doubt derived from how little they must know in order to impress someone with their language abilities.

Third, whereas learning a first language is a relatively unproblematic endeavor for typically developing children, second-language acquisition is a much riskier business in which individual characteristics may well play a large part. The follow-

ing factors have all been proposed as making a difference in second-language acquisition:

1. **An aptitude factor** Some people are more talented as second-language learners.
2. **A social factor** Some people are more outgoing and more willing to take risks as second-language learners.
3. **A psychological factor** Some people are more motivated because they want to become like the people who speak the language they are trying to learn.

In assessing the progress that an individual child is making in a second language it may be necessary to take some or all of these factors into consideration.

WHAT PRESCHOOL EDUCATORS NEED TO KNOW ABOUT SECOND-LANGUAGE LEARNING

Given what is known about first-language development and about the differences between first- and second-language acquisition, what do preschool educators need to know in order to be able to meet the challenge of making the preschool educational experience as optimal as possible for second-language–learning children? The goal of this book is to answer the following questions:

1. *What are the social and linguistic factors that affect a child whose home language is not English when that child comes to a preschool classroom where English is used?*

    When children from homes in which English is not the home language begin attending a preschool classroom in which English is one of the languages being used, they will need to adjust to a new social and linguistic situation. Chapter 2 discusses what this means for these children in terms of social and linguistic constraints.

2. *What is the likely path of development for a young child learning a second language?*

    There is a different developmental path taken by young second-language learners than that for first-language learners. Preschool educators will need to know what this developmental path is in order to be able to observe, plan, assess, and serve second-language learning children. Chapters 3 and 4 discuss this developmental path, and Chapter 5 discusses individual differences among young second-language learners.

3. *What is the teacher's role, and what can be done in the classroom for second-language–learning children?*

    The teacher's role in the preschool classroom that includes second-language–learning children will need to be broadened to include ways of communicating with these children as well as ways to adjust the curriculum in order to be as responsive to their needs as possible. Chapters 6 and 7 discuss classroom-based strategies for working with second-language–learning children.

4. *What can teachers tell parents about what they can do to help?*

    Parents of second-language–learning children will have many questions about their child's developmental progress, in language as well as in all other areas. They may have questions about the child's social isolation in the classroom, the possibility of first-language loss, the perceived need to learn English rapidly, the next stage of their children's education, and a myriad of other concerns. Chapter 8 provides strategies for helping parents understand the importance of these issues and for mapping out ways to help parents make decisions that will benefit their children.

5. *How can preschool educators tell when intervention is necessary with a second-language–learning child?*

   Preschool educators are often called upon to assess whether a child's behavior warrants further investigation for intervention. Because communicative factors related to language affect children's social behavior, it is often difficult for preschool educators to know whether certain behaviors in second-language–learning children are indicative of true developmental delay or are merely due to the pressures of the new social environment to which the children are being exposed. Chapter 9 discusses the ways in which teachers and administrators can assess the needs of these children.

6. *What does this information about the second-language–learning process for young children mean for effective preschool programs?*

   Chapter 10 discusses the ways in which this information fits with the recommendations of the National Association for the Education of Young Children (NAEYC) concerning responses to linguistic and cultural diversity.

SOURCES OF INFORMATION ABOUT SECOND-LANGUAGE–LEARNING CHILDREN

A variety of sources of information is used in answering these questions, including previous studies by other researchers and classroom observations and interviews with teachers, parents, and administrators conducted by the author. One of the primary sources of information about what occurs in a classroom with young second-language learners is a study I conducted over 2 years in an English-language nursery school classroom (Tabors, 1984, 1987; Tabors & Snow, 1994). A brief description of the classroom, the teachers, the children, and my role in the classroom follows in order to provide context for the discussion of much of the classroom information in the book.

The Classroom Setting

The setting for the study was an English-language nursery school classroom located on the second floor of a high-rise apartment building at a local university. The apartment building was used by the university for married graduate student housing, and many families from outside the United States lived in the building and sent their children to the nursery school. All of the families whose children attended the center had some affiliation with the university.

The Teachers

The teachers in the classroom during the study were Marion, the head teacher; Rosa, the assistant teacher the first year; and Joanne, the assistant teacher the second year. Marion was an experienced preschool educator. In an interview, Marion mentioned that she considered her way of running a classroom as being halfway between the extremes of very open and very structured. From my observations I would say that she was a confident teacher with a highly verbal style who related well to the students on a very adult level.

Rosa, the assistant teacher during the first year of the study, was a native Spanish speaker who came to the United States from Cuba when she was 11 years old. Her interactions with the children were relaxed and playful. She was a frequent leader of circle time, and she was clever at getting and holding the children's attention.

Joanne, the assistant teacher during the second year of the study, was very involved in the children's activities and was a frequent participant in their play. She often adopted a lightly teasing or playful technique with the children, which delighted the children and made her very popular in the classroom.

The Children

There were 15 children in the classroom at any one time. The children ranged in age from 2 years 9 months to 5 years old at the beginning of the school year. The children from the nursery school who appear in this book are listed in alphabetical order in Table 2.

As can be seen in Table 2, the children who were learning English as a second language came from a variety of countries and home-language backgrounds. Because of this variety, it was unusual to hear children using their home languages in the classroom, although it was certainly not discouraged by the teachers. Except for the Korean girls, who did on occasion form their own play group, most of the children found playmates and activities that placed them in circumstances in which English was the primary language being used.

Inside the Classroom

The nursery school classroom was a large room with windows all along one side overlooking the playground. The room was divided into several areas that served different purposes: the block area, the house area, the bench, the puzzle table, the art or project tables, and the water/sand table.

The block area was located in one corner of the room along the side with the windows. It was a carpeted area used for all group activities as well as a building area for blocks. The blocks were kept in the bookcases that divided the block area from the house area. Also available in the block area were toy trains and

Table 2.   Children in the English-language nursery school classroom over the 2-year study

Name[a]	Sex	Place of origin	Home language
Akemi	F	Japan	Japanese
Andrew	M	United States	English
Byong-sun	M	Korea	Korean
Elena	F	USSR	Russian
James	M	United States	English
Jennifer	F	United States	English
Jessica	F	United States	English
Kaori	F	Japan	Japanese
Kumiko	F	Japan	Japanese
Leandro	M	Brazil	Portuguese
Ling Ling	F	Taiwan	Taiwanese
Matthew	M	United States	English
Miguel	M	Puerto Rico	Spanish
Myong	F	Korea	Korean
Naoshi	M	Japan	Japanese
Natalie	F	United States	English
Pierre	M	France	French
Poram	F	Korea	Korean
Rebecca	F	United States	English
Sally	F	United States	English
Sook-whan	F	Korea	Korean
Supat	M	Thailand	Thai
Taro	M	Japan	Japanese

[a]The children's names have been changed.

tracks, large toy trucks and buses, people figures, and plastic toy animals.

The house area occupied the other corner of the room along the window side. This area contained a large wooden structure that served as a playhouse underneath and a loft area above that was reached by climbing a ladder. The playhouse was furnished with child-size kitchen equipment and a table and chairs; the loft was furnished with pillows and books. Also available in this area was a full-length mirror and a large collection of dress-up clothes.

Opposite the house, attached to a central column that divided the room in half, was a bed area and a storage area for more books. Along one wall of the playhouse was a carpeted bench. Near the bench there was a large round table that was often used for puzzles or other similar manipulative activities. Along the wall behind the puzzle table were shelves where puzzles, Legos, and other games were stored.

There were two other rectangular tables in the classroom that were used for art or other projects during the free play period and for snack and lunch later in the morning. Typical activities at these tables included playing with playdough, drawing, and painting. Along the inside wall of the classroom was the water/sand table that could be used for play when filled with water or sand but acted as a storage surface when not otherwise in use.

The overall feeling of the room was of a bright, pleasant environment decorated primarily with the children's own artwork and set up in a fashion similar to many other nursery school classrooms.

Organization of Classroom Time

The first 1½ hours in the morning was a free play period. During this time children were typically offered a group of options from which to choose. Several projects might be put out on the activity tables, such as Legos, playdough, or drawing equipment, or a special project (e.g., pizza making) might be organized by one of the teachers. Children also had free access to the block and house areas during the free play periods and could develop their own play activities as well. Most of the children moved freely around the room, choosing first one kind of activity and then another depending on what interested them at the moment. The teachers

作述，預告．

guided children in their choices if they seemed to be undecided and made sure that all of the children had completed a project if it was meant as an "all class" project.

A brief cleanup period followed free play. Cleanup time was heralded with a cleanup song, and the teachers helped children put away toys and other activities that had been used during the free play period. This was followed by circle time.

For circle, all the children gathered on the carpet in the block area. Circle time usually began with the children joining hands and singing a song together. After this they sat down on the rug and followed the lead of the teacher in singing songs, playing games, or naming colors and shapes as a group. After circle time, the children washed their hands and sat down for snack, choosing their own location at one of the three tables. When children completed their snacks, they went to the cubby area and got ready to go outside to the playground.

Out in the playground there was a variety of activities from which to choose. There were swings to swing on, structures to climb on, and bikes to ride.

After coming back inside, the children again came to the carpeted area for story time. During this time one of the teachers would read aloud from a book, alternately reading and displaying the pictures from the book to the group, frequently asking questions about the story as she read. When the book reading was completed, the children were dismissed from the area to collect their lunchboxes and settle down at one of the three tables for lunch.

After lunch, the children either went back outside or remained in the classroom to play until they were picked up to go home.

Participant Observation

In order to develop a complete picture of how young children go about the process of acquiring a second language, I spent several mornings a week for 2 years in this nursery school classroom, observing, taking notes, and audiotaping the children's and teachers' interactions. My role in the classroom was that of a *participant observer*; that is, someone who was slightly apart from the everyday life of the classroom but still functioned as a member of the group. Interestingly, the children seemed to accept this role without much question. When I separated myself from the children and concentrated on taking notes, they did not interrupt me and would proceed in their play as if I were not in the room. When I made myself available by putting down my notebook, the children would approach me for help or conversation much as they would the teachers in the classroom.

Occasionally a child would ask what I was doing when I was taking notes. Leandro was one of the few children who asked me a direct question about the note taking. I was taking notes during a conversation I was having with Leandro one day, and he asked, "What you are writing?" I said, "I'm writing what you are saying." Then he looked out the window and said, "Police car." Then he looked at me and said, "You write police car?" I said, "Yes." This type of direct questioning was, however, quite unusual. On the whole, I found that it was very easy to move back and forth between interactions with the children and teachers (participant) and note taking (observer) without jeopardizing either role. By being a participant I came to know all of the children and the teachers; by being an observer I was able to record interactions that might have otherwise gone unnoticed. At the end of each day of observation I typed up my notes and my personal interpretations of what I was observing. In this way, I developed an extensive record of the activities in the classroom. Much of the information and most of the examples that follow about second-language learning in a preschool educational setting come from this record.

part one

The Second-Language–Learning Child's Task

chapter two

Two Portraits
Juliana and Byong-sun

When young children from non–English-speaking homes first arrive in a preschool education setting in which English is used, they will have to cope with a variety of social and linguistic demands that children from English-speaking homes will not have to face. The first section of this chapter presents a portrait of an English-speaking child during a free play period in her preschool classroom, noting the social and linguistic competencies that she displays in her interactions with her classmates. The second section follows a Korean child during a similar period in his English-language classroom, noting the social and linguistic constraints on his interactions with his classmates. The final section relates the social and linguistic constraints faced by second-language–learning children to a particular theory of social dominance.

PORTRAIT OF JULIANA

I visited Juliana's nursery school classroom in a large midwestern city one afternoon in October. Juliana and her classmates were 4 years of age, and their classroom was similar to the English-language classroom I had previously studied. The classroom was a large room broken into areas with structures and bookcases, with an entire wall of glass looking out over the playground outside. A lengthy free play period occurred during the afternoon, and Juliana agreed to wear a small Minnie Mouse backpack with an audiotape recorder inside as she played. After a few minutes, Juliana appeared to have forgotten she was wearing the backpack on her back and unhesitatingly entered into the play with the other children. I followed Juliana and took field notes as she played with her friends.

Juliana at Play

Although this was a free play period, it followed a brief lesson that the student teacher, Wendy, had presented to the children as part of a unit on airplanes. This lesson had included a short film about stunt pilots and their tricks, and props, such as a pilot's hat, gloves, and goggles, were available in the classroom from previous lessons during the week. During the free play period, Wendy encouraged the children to build an airplane out of large wooden blocks and to take the airplane on a trip.

As free play began, however, Juliana was most interested in being in the dress-up area. She and her friend Ellen began to negotiate over the roles they would play. First Juliana informed Ellen, "I don't want to be the kitty." So Ellen offered, "I will." Then Juliana announced, "And I'll be the mommy." Ellen replied, "I'll be the m . . . , I'll be the big sister." Then Susan came into the dress-up area and entered the negotiations as well. "I'll be the mommy, too," she offered.

Having sorted out their roles and collected some baby dolls from the dress-up corner, the three girls walked over to the block area where Wendy was organizing the building of the airplane with large wooden blocks for seats. Susan suggested to Juliana, "You be the pilot, okay?" But Juliana demurred, "No-o-o-o." Wendy asked, "What would you like to be, Juliana?" "I don't want to be the pilot," she replied. Wendy persisted, "You don't want to be the pilot? Do you want to be a passenger?" Juliana shook her head "no." Then Ellen offered, "I want to be a passenger," and Wendy quickly agreed, "Okay." Then Juliana decided, "I want to sit on one of these seats." "Okay," said Wendy, "and let's put the seats in the plane." "Can I sit on that too?" asked Ellen. "Yes," replied Wendy, and then reiterated, "and let's put the seats on the plane."

Having arranged a few blocks for seats, Ellen and Juliana climbed into the airplane with Ellen suggesting, "Juliana, let's sit next to each other back here." But Juliana wanted to sit closer to the front of the plane, so she announced, "I'm going to sit here." Then Ellen changed her mind and joined Juliana saying, "I have to sit next to you. You know why? 'Cuz you're coming to my house."

Meanwhile, Wendy was talking with Susan. "Where are we going to go visit on our trip? Do you remember what city you drew on your map yesterday?" After further discussion about their destination, Wendy asked Ellen and Juliana, "You guys, you want to go visit Florida with Susan and me?" They enthusiastically agreed.

It was soon clear, however, that the flight was not yet ready to get off the ground. Susan hopped out of the plane saying, "I'm going to get some dishes," and Ellen followed her announcing, "I'm going to get the drinkies." After both Ellen and Susan returned to the plane with the dishes and cups, Wendy asked, "We've got to get some seat belts, don't we?" Ellen answered, "Oh, we forgot to get them on." Juliana reached out to take a seat belt from Wendy who was pulling them out of a box near the plane. "That's going to be mine," Juliana said. Then she and Ellen spent a few minutes arranging dishes, cups, and seat belts near their seats on the upturned blocks. Ellen handed Juliana a cup. Juliana replied, "Thank you." Then Ellen decided that she did not need a seat belt. She announced, "I don't need one." Juliana followed suit, "I don't need one either."

Ellen then announced, "My baby needs a bottle," and exited the plane in search of a bottle from the dress-up area. Wendy offered a seat belt to Susan, but she picked up one of the rejected seat belts that Ellen and Juliana had dropped on the floor. Then Juliana decided that her baby should not be left unprotected and announced, "My baby needs a seat belt," three times until Wendy heard her and handed her a new one saying, "Here you go."

Ellen returned to the plane and upon seeing that Juliana's baby had a seat belt, requested one for her baby from Wendy, who handed her one and then asked, "Do we have everything we need?" Ellen replied, "Yeah," but Susan contradicted her, "Not ye-e-e-t." Wendy queried her, "Not yet?" Susan replied, "My baby needs a seat belt too." Wendy answered, "She does?" But Juliana suggested, "Let her sit with my baby, all right?" Susan rejected this idea, "No." Juliana tried again, "I'll be really friendly." Wendy intervened and suggested, "Maybe she can sit with her a little bit later. How's that?" "When we get back, she can sit with me and my little baby, all right?" decided Juliana.

Then Juliana announced to Ellen that they needed to go back to the dress-up area. They returned to the plane in high-heel shoes, and Juliana announced, "I have my pretty shoes on. These are my shoes." After climbing back into the plane, Juliana suggested, "Ellen, let's pretend these are my shoes, okay?" Ellen then proposed an identity switch. "And then let's pretend my name's Juliana and your name's Ellen." Then Susan chimed in, "And pretend my name's . . ." "Dorothy," supplied Juliana. Susan echoed, "Dorothy."

Juliana and Ellen announced their new identities to Wendy. Ellen told her, "I'm Juliana," and Juliana told her, "I'm Ellen and these are my shoes. And she's Juliana, so she's wearing those shoes." Playing along with this switch, Wendy asked, "Ellen, how did your hair get so light?" "I don't know why," answered Juliana. Then Juliana, while pointing to Ellen, told Wendy, "She's Juliana." Wendy obligingly said, "Juliana, your hair got so dark. Are you wearing a wig? No?"

Then Juliana announced some bad news to Ellen, "I can't go. My baby's sick." Then she told Wendy, "I can't go. Know why? 'Cuz my baby has some allergies. She has a fever. So she can't go to Florida." Susan, still intent on the trip to Florida, said, "My baby can go to Florida." But Juliana reiterated, "Because my baby has some allergies and she has a fever." So Ellen suggested, "We need to drop off our babies, right?" Juliana agreed, "Right." Wendy asked, "How are they going to get all better?" Juliana replied, "We have to give them some medicine." Susan then decided that her baby was also sick. And Juliana graciously conceded, "Yeah, you can come with us. But first you have to take your seat belt off." As the girls began to leave the plane, Wendy asked, "And they're not going to go to Florida with us?" Juliana replied, "No, my baby can't come, but when she takes her temperature, she can come."

Then Ellen and Juliana adopted baby voices and announced, "I'm not sick anymore . . . I'm not sick anymore." Juliana told Wendy, "She's not sick anymore, so now she can go." Wendy replied, "Oh, great. Should I open up the door?" "Yeah," said Ellen and Juliana and they climbed back into the plane. Ellen announced, "Juliana and I are going to be in the way back." Then Wendy said, "I guess I should get on, huh?"

Susan asked, "How long is it going to take?" Wendy replied, "I don't know. How long does the flight to Florida take?" Susan suggested, "A day." Ellen suggested, "Ten minutes." Susan decided, "Forty-five minutes. My watch says forty-five minutes. One, two, three, four, BLAST OFF!" But Juliana was not ready. "No! My baby needs to go back. My baby has a temperature now." Wendy announced, "Oh no. We've got to have an emergency landing. "Everybody fasten their seat belts for an emergency landing!" Juliana then ran from the plane, instructing, "Don't do the plane until we're back!" Wendy replied, "We'll keep it warming up." Returning to the plane, Juliana announced, "My baby's better." Wendy answered, "She's better? Are we going to go on our flight?" Juliana conceded, "Yup."

But now it was time for a few last minute provisions. Susan brought a bag of chips. Then Ellen mentioned that they needed flowers and went and got some from another part of the room. Then Juliana said, "Wait! Everybody needs hats" and went off to get some from the dress-up area. Wendy decided to wear the pilot's hat, saying, "I want this one. If I'm going to be the pilot I want my hat back on. I need my gloves too, don't I?" Then everyone settled into their seats again and looked for their seat belts. Wendy asked again, "Are we about ready for takeoff?" Everyone chorused, "Yeah!" Susan again announced, "Forty-five minutes." And Wendy reiterated, "Forty-five minutes to Florida." Finally Susan announced, "All right, we're there!"

Soon after arrival in Florida, the free play period ended and the travelers busily dismantled the plane and put the blocks away.

Social and Linguistic Aspects of Juliana's Play

During this free play period, Juliana demonstrates a variety of linguistic and social competencies that make her an active participant. At the very beginning, she is able to enter into negotiations concerning roles. Then she indicates her willingness to be part of the sociodramatic play by declaring where she wants to sit, although she rejects the starring role of pilot and even the lesser role of passenger. This independent move results in a concession on Ellen's part, as she moves to sit with Juliana, after Juliana rejects Ellen's suggestion to sit with her.

A period of constant flow of talk and suggestions among Wendy, Susan, Ellen, and Juliana follows as they develop the airplane theme. During this time, Juliana has to make the same bid three times to get the seat belt she believes is needed for her baby, but she persists until Wendy hears her and fulfills her request.

Juliana is then involved in an unsuccessful exchange with Susan during which she tries to persuade Susan to have their babies sit together. Eventually Wendy intervenes with a suggestion to put off a decision at this point, and Juliana proposes a final solution for "when we get back."

After the identity switch incident, Juliana twice takes control of the direction of the play, first by announcing that her baby is sick and then by forcing an emergency landing when the baby's illness recurs. Both of these suggestions are powerful moves on her part and are taken up by the other participants as vital elements in the play. She is even able to keep everyone waiting, until she declares that her baby is better and the flight can proceed.

During this free play episode, then, it can be readily seen how Juliana uses linguistic and social moves that establish and maintain her position as a full-fledged participant in the ongoing play. She uses language to negotiate, reject, persuade, bid for attention, and make suggestions, all within the flow of the play activity. Although not all of her bids or suggestions are successful, she is clearly a major player in the developing scenario and is able to use her skills to be heard and to help fashion the direction of the play.

PORTRAIT OF BYONG-SUN

Byong-sun was a 4-year-old Korean boy who began coming to the English-language nursery school classroom in the second year of my study. One November morning, I followed Byong-sun everywhere he went during the free play period at the beginning of the day and wrote field notes about his activities.

Byong-sun at Play

When Byong-sun arrived in the classroom, he immediately went to the circle table and sat down where Legos were available in boxes that were open but not emptied out. He started to remove some pieces from the boxes. Jessica approached the circle table with her mother. She sat down and began manipulating a few pieces that were on the table. Byong-sun did not pay any attention and kept playing, humming to himself. Jessica's mother reached in front of Byong-sun to get a few more pieces for Jessica. Byong-sun protested mildly by making a noise that sounded like "unhuhn." Then Jessica's mother moved the whole box closer to Jessica. But Jessica was not particularly interested in playing with the Legos, and she soon got up and left, followed by her mother. This left Byong-sun alone at the table. He continued his play, taking some more pieces out of the box and singing aloud.

As he played with the Legos, Byong-sun occasionally looked over at the next table where a group of children was playing with playdough. Eventually he got up from the table and went over to the sink area where there was a box full of playdough implements including molds and knives. He knelt down on the floor and started rummaging through the box. He picked a knife out of the collection and held it in his left hand, while he continued to explore the contents of the box with his right hand. At this point he looked over at the table where the other children were playing with the playdough and then started to get up, stopped, knelt down again, and resumed his search in the box.

Next, Byong-sun looked up at me where I was still sitting at the circle table and made a requesting noise (a whining tone with rising intonation). I did not respond, but Marion, who had spotted Byong-sun on the floor, did respond. She came over and asked him a series of questions. "What are you looking for, Byong-sun? What is it that you need? You have a knife. What else are you looking for? Are you looking for a rolling pin?" "Yeah," answered Byong-sun. "It looks to me like all the rolling pins are out. We'll have to get some more so we don't have to share," she concluded. Then Marion left with a child who wanted her help in another part of the room.

Byong-sun took the knife he had gotten out of the box and went over to the playdough table, sitting down at an empty seat where there was a large glob of playdough and a roller. He began to roll out the playdough with the roller. The other children at the table, Sally, Rebecca, and Ling Ling, were making birthday cakes, talking about what they were doing as they played. Byong-sun did not join in their conversation and looked down as he rolled out the playdough in front of him. Then he looked up and listened to the other children at the table as they talked, holding a ball of playdough in his hand.

Next, Byong-sun looked over at the sand table where Naoshi, Andrew, and James were playing. He got up from the table, went to the sink, washed his hands, took a paper towel to dry his hands, threw the paper towel in the garbage can, and went to the sand table.

When he arrived at the sand table, Byong-sun tried to establish himself next to James, but James protested, blocking Byong-sun's access to the table. Andrew told James that it would be all right to let Byong-sun have a place. Rebecca also arrived at the table and pushed her way into the group. Byong-sun took up a position at the end of the table, picked up a long-handled spoon, and began filling up and dumping out a small frying pan with sand.

Andrew said, "Let's make a road." Naoshi, Andrew, and James became involved in working on the sand at their end of the table. Byong-sun brushed some sand off his hand, patted the sand in front of him, and sang a bit to himself. Next, Byong-sun took the frying pan full of sand and threw some sand into the middle of the table, while looking at James. This did not get a response. He did it again. Still his action received no response. Byong-sun banged his spoon on an orange juice container near James. James did not notice. Then Byong-sun filled an orange juice container that Naoshi had been using. Naoshi also did not notice.

James and Rebecca then started working on the sand mound to form a birthday cake, as Rebecca talked about today being Ling Ling's birthday. Then James sang "Happy Birthday to You" quietly. Byong-sun dumped out the sand in the frying pan and started scooping again. Then he held up the frying pan toward Rebecca, but did not say anything. She did not respond in any way. Andrew came back to the table and said to Rebecca, "Be nice to Ling Ling today, right?"

At this point Matthew came in with his mother. His mother tried to get Matthew interested in the sand activity by picking up the long-handled spoon. Byong-sun immediately protested very clearly, "No, Byong-sun's." Matthew's mom put the spoon down and tried to mediate between Matthew and Myong who did not want him on her side of the table. Byong-sun alternated between watching this drama and working on the sand in front of him.

Byong-sun picked up the long-handled spoon and put the handle through a funnel. Then he withdrew it and patted the sand mound with it. At this point, Rebecca reached for the spoon and said, "I need this, okay?" and took it away from Byong-sun without protest. Next, Myong took the funnel that Byong-sun had been playing with and added that to the sand mound; then Myong grabbed the frying pan from him and added that to the

"cake." This left Byong-sun with nothing to play with. He put his thumb between his front teeth and watched the other children as they continued to work on the sand mound.

Myong called to Marion to show off their accomplishment. She came and commented that it was great except for the fact that it was beginning to spill over the edge. At this moment, Rebecca reached over to collect the sand from in front of Byong-sun to put it on the mound. Byong-sun said, "Get out!" and gave Rebecca a good push with his hip. Rebecca turned to Marion to complain, "He said 'get out.'" Marion interpreted this to mean that Byong-sun wanted to get out from behind the table, so she told Rebecca to just let him by. But when Rebecca moved aside and Marion encouraged Byong-sun to come out, he did not move. Then Marion realized that Byong-sun did not have any more sand to play with, and she encouraged the other children to spread the sand out again so everyone could share.

Marion then went to get one of the guinea pigs out of his cage so that the children could take turns holding him. Byong-sun followed the group that moved over to the chairs set up in front of the guinea pig cages. Marion saw that Byong-sun had joined the group and asked, "Byong-sun, would you like a turn, too?" He nodded his head "yes." Then Marion said, "Byong-sun, would you like to sit and watch?" And he sat down opposite Matthew who was already holding the guinea pig, smiling at Matthew as he did so. Marion gave Byong-sun a piece of carrot for the guinea pig. Matthew reached out and took the carrot away from Byong-sun and gave it to the guinea pig. Then Byong-sun knelt down and petted the guinea pig on Matthew's lap.

Then Marion announced, "Now it's Byong-sun's turn." She sat down next to Byong-sun and helped lift the guinea pig off of Matthew's lap and onto Byong-sun's, but Byong-sun was not happy with the guinea pig on his lap, so Marion took it on her lap and let Byong-sun pet him. When the guinea pig shook himself, Byong-sun laughed. Marion remarked, "He likes gentle petting." Byong-sun said, "No." Marion replied, "Yes, he does." After some more petting, Marion said to Byong-sun, "You could go and see if Rebecca wanted a turn," but Byong-sun made no move to leave.

Then Sally came over to the group to hold the guinea pig. Byong-sun stayed seated on a chair nearby. A piece of carrot was on the floor. Sally leaned toward it but could not reach. She looked up at Byong-sun, who picked it up and handed it to her. She said, "Thank you." A minute later I asked Sally if she had had enough holding and she said she had, so I took the guinea pig, let Byong-sun say good-bye to him, and then put him in the cage.

Once the guinea pig was back in his cage, Byong-sun went to the block area where Rebecca, Ling Ling, Sally, Leandro, and Andrew were playing. When Byong-sun came into the block area, Andrew was playing with the pop push toy (a push toy with balls inside that pop up). As Byong-sun arrived, Andrew dropped the toy and went off. Byong-sun picked it up and began pushing it around in an area where the other children were not playing. Byong-sun pushed the toy over to me and pointed at one of the animals inside the plastic top, saying something I was unable to understand. I said, "What's that?" He answered, "It's a bear." Then he pushed the toy out of the block area and around to the house area. Here he found Taro alone with the busy box (a toy with figures that pop up when released from a trap door).

Taro looked up from the busy box as Byong-sun came near and said something to him. Byong-sun replied "No" as he sat down near the busy box. Taro tried to play with the busy box, but Byong-sun said "No" again. Then Byong-sun turned the box so that it was facing him, and he began playing with it as Taro sat and watched. Then Byong-sun started to pop up the different creatures that appear out of the box. He turned and verbalized to Taro, but when Taro moved nearer, Byong-sun put up his arm and said, "No!" Taro stopped and sat behind Byong-sun watching him play. After popping up one of the figures, Byong-sun looked up at me and said, "Look at the bear." Then he popped up another and asked, "What's that?" I said, "Dog?" He said, "Yeah." Then he went on to identify the "mommy" and "daddy" figures. Then he exclaimed over the "doggie" and said "Look at the bear" again. Then Byong-sun noticed the numbers written along the bottom of the box. He counted aloud in English from one to five as he followed the numbers on the box. The next time he popped up the bear, he turned to Taro and made claws and growled at him. Then he turned back to the box and played for awhile longer with Taro still sitting behind watching. Then Taro picked up the pop push toy and went away. Byong-sun continued with the busy box until cleanup time was announced.

Social and Linguistic Constraints in Byong-sun's Play

In this description of how Byong-sun spends his time during the free play period, it is apparent that he is quite socially isolated from the rest of his classmates. For part of the free play period, he works alone with Lego pieces that have been left on a table where he can use them without having to ask for help. When he chooses to join a group, he finds a seat that is unoccupied at the play-dough table or, with some difficulty, works himself into a location that is available at the sand table. When he tries to get the attention of the other children, he is mostly ignored. He rarely protests when he is being taken advantage of. Only three times during the free play period does he defend himself, twice with adults and a third time when an adult is nearby to mediate. The only child who accords him any deference is Taro, who is also a second-language learner and considerably younger than Byong-sun. On the whole, Byong-sun was being treated as a socially irrelevant member of the class.

In the portrait of Byong-sun it is also possible to see the linguistic constraints he must face. Because he is a second-language learner, Byong-sun has a highly limited repertoire to choose from in communicative situations. When he is unable to find what he is looking for in the box under the sink, he uses a generic whine to indicate to me that he needs help. But when a helpful adult arrives, he is unable to tell her what it is he wants and she has to try to guess. In one of the situations when he protests being taken advantage of, he uses a phrase ("Get out") that he has probably heard other children use and has applied it to his situation, although it is not quite right and, therefore, is misinterpreted. Several other times, when he does try to communicate verbally, he is not understood.

There are times, however, when Byong-sun is able to show his competence in English, as when he names the figures and counts the numbers on the busy box. In this situation, he is in charge and is setting the communicative agenda, showing off what he knows and even turning my "What's that?" question around to have me identify one of the figures on the box. It is in this low-pressure situation that Byong-sun demonstrates the greatest proficiency in his new language.

This portrait of Byong-sun demonstrates the classic *double bind* that anyone who is learning a new language must face: In order to learn this new language, Byong-sun must be socially accepted by those who speak the language; but to be socially accepted, he must already be able to speak the new language. In other words, in any language-learning situation in natural circumstances, communicative competence and social competence are inextricably interrelated; the double bind is that each is necessary for the development of the other.

OMEGA CHILDREN

Classrooms constitute a particular social setting, and the social setting in the classroom is not just the background context for the second-language–learning children's language-learning experience, but is, instead, an integral part of that experience. In fact, Byong-sun's behavior as detailed in the previous portrait, and the reaction of the other children to Byong-sun, can be seen as strongly related to a social dominance theory that has been developed by Garnica (1983). This theory explores the possibility that some children—*omega children*—are socially ineffective because they lack communicative as well as social competence.

Garnica's (1983) study focused on six kindergarten children who were identified through sociometric means as being rated at the bottom of the social hierarchy in their classrooms. These children were compared with six other children in the same classrooms selected at random and matched for sex. Social interactions of these children were recorded in the classroom context, and three 20-minute samples were analyzed for each of the 12 children using a variety of comparison measures. The results, all of which were statistically significant, were as follows:

> The omega children were observed to engage in fewer child–child conversations with different partners and to produce fewer conversational turns . . . The differences were so marked for the omega/non-omega groups that the distributions for the two groups did not even overlap in these comparisons. The same lack of overlap in group comparisons held for measures of the number of conversation initiations that were directed to the target child and the frequency with which the child's name was used by the other children . . . during the play periods observed. Thus, the omega child does not seem to participate in verbal interactions with many other children in the group and even those exchanges that do occur are of short duration.
>
> Furthermore, the omega children are hardly ever addressed by other children . . . The range is 0–2 times for the omega children as opposed to 9–16 times for non-omega, which may partly explain why the omega child's name is heard considerably less frequently in the course of the verbal chatter in child–child conversations. The amount of private speech exhibited by the omega children is much greater than that exhibited by the non-omega children. (Garnica, 1983, pp. 240–241).

In her discussion concerning these children, Garnica comments:

> The emerging picture of the omega child seems to be one of a verbally neglected individual. Hardly any of the other children appear intentionally to engage the omega child in conversations and the omega child only infrequently initiates verbal exchanges with other children. The conversational partner network of the omega

weaker or reduce

child is drastically limited and thus the amount of speech that the child produces in productive, interactive social exchanges with other children is highly attenuated.

Interestingly, the omega child is not often silent. S/he produces a variety of verbalizations but these verbalizations consist of long self-directed narratives or conversations with pretend conversational partners and are ignored by the other children.

All of these features present the omega child as a verbally neglected and isolated member of the group . . . In light of these circumstances the omega child appears totally unrepresented in the verbal activity. This child produces vocalizations that are clearly not intended for anyone other than self. (Garnica, 1983, p. 241).

The overall picture, then, of the omega child is one who is ignored by his or her peers and is socially ineffective in interaction situations. But how does this situation arise in the first place?

Garnica (1983) does not attempt to answer this question in her analysis, but she does present evidence of interactions with omega and non-omega children that suggests that communicative competence or, in this case, communicative incompetence, may be a contributing factor in how the omega children are treated by their peers. In a discussion of an interaction sequence in which an omega child attempts to procure a pink Magic Marker from another child, Garnica mentions that, although the omega child uses the same "bidding" system as non-omega children in this situation, the omega child is not forceful (she hints rather than requests) nor does she use nonverbal communication (i.e., raising her hand) in conjunction with her bid. In other words, her communicative competence (doing it correctly both verbally and nonverbally) in this situation is not sufficiently developed to achieve the desired end product: use of the pink Magic Marker.

But, comments Garnica (1983), what if she had "done it right"? Would she have gotten the pink Magic Marker? The answer here is apparently also no, this time because of the child's status as a socially incompetent individual. The rule seems to be that if an omega child does not behave forcefully, she will not get what she wants; however, if she does behave forcefully she will be ridiculed or teased by the other members of the social group and still will not get what she wants. It seems evident, then, that communicative competence and social competence are so closely related for these omega children that it is not possible to sort out primary from secondary factors. If a child is not a good communicator, people will ignore him or her, and if people ignore the child, it is hard to get into social situations in which he or she could become a better communicator.

This, of course, is precisely the situation in which children whose home language is other than English find themselves during the first few months in preschool education settings in which English is used. Automatically, because of their lack of language proficiency, they are extensively ignored by the English-speaking children in the classroom, who treat them as if they are invisible, do not initiate communications with them, and often ignore their attempts at initiation, just as the children in the nursery school did with Byong-sun. Second-language–learning children are relegated to the bottom of the social heap right from the start.

Because of this situation, second-language–learning children like Byong-sun are left alone much of the time at first. They may spend their time playing alone silently, or humming, singing, or talking to themselves—very much the same portrait as was painted of the omega children previously. In interaction situations, these children wait for the other person to be the initiator, and they rarely presume to try to get one of the other children to do something for them; if there is something they want, they do it themselves or they do without. These features also make second-language–learning children look a lot like the description of the omega children. And, in fact, for at least the first few months in a preschool education setting, second-language–learning children are, indeed, omega children. But, fortunately, most of them do not remain omega children. What makes it possible for second-language–learning children to eventually escape this double bind? Chapters 3 and 4 discuss the process of second-language acquisition for these young children and show how it is possible for second-language–learners to gain enough facility with their new language to become social members of the group and to use their social skills to get into group situations where they will be able to hear, understand, and then begin to use their new language as well.

chapter three

Getting Started in a Second Language

When young children whose home language is not English first arrive in a classroom where English is one of the languages used, they are at the starting point of a new developmental pathway, a pathway that leads to the development of skills in a second language. Although there will be differences in the way that children pursue learning a second language, researchers have noted a consistent developmental sequence for young children:

1. There may be a period of time when children continue to use their home languages in the second-language situation.
2. When they discover that their home language does not work in this situation, children enter a nonverbal period as they collect information about the new language and perhaps spend some time in sound experimentation.
3. Children begin to go public, using individual words and phrases in the new language.
4. Children begin to develop productive use of the second language.

This chapter discusses the first two periods in this developmental sequence for second-language learners. Chapter 4 discusses the second two periods, and individual differences in this developmental process is the topic of Chapter 5.

HOME-LANGUAGE USE

When young children find themselves in a social situation in which those around them speak a different language, there are really only two options: They can continue to speak the language they already know, or they can stop talking altogether.

Some children initially pursue the first of these options. In my study I observed a Brazilian boy, Leandro, during his first day in the English-language classroom, where no one else spoke Portuguese, his home language. At lunch, Leandro tried some yogurt and then pushed it away telling me something in Portuguese, which must have involved an explanation for why he was not going to eat it. After lunch he asked Joanna a definite question in Portuguese. She shook her head and said she did not understand. Later he asked me a question in Portuguese. I also said I did not understand. He did not seem distressed, but he did not get an answer either.

Naoshi, a Japanese child in the same classroom, limited his efforts to the other Asian children. During the first few days in class he tried to speak Japanese to Ling Ling, who was Taiwanese, and Byong-sun, who was Korean; neither of them could respond to him in Japanese. In both Leandro's and Naoshi's cases, unsuccessful initial efforts apparently convinced these children that they would not be understood if they used their home language and, therefore, each discontinued the attempt to speak it in the classroom.

Some children, however, have been observed to persist for a considerably longer period of time in the use of their home language in second-language situations. In a study involving 40 second-language–learning children ranging in age from 18 months to 12 years, Saville-Troike (1987) found that 3- to 7-year-old children were willing to engage in what she terms *dilingual discourse* for some time after arriving in a setting in which a different language was spoken. By dilingual discourse, Saville-Troike means that the children continued to speak their home language as if those around them could understand them. In fact, those around them often did answer them, using, of course, the language that the children could not understand. Saville-Troike reports that this form of communication

> Was generally effective for achieving desired ends when the children were involved in play, especially when there were objects to be manipulated. When context alone did not suffice for meaning to be inferred, however, the response to an unintelligible verbalization was frequently a blank look. (pp. 84–85)

The older children in Saville-Troike's (1987) study came to the realization quite quickly that this form of communication would not work; however, two younger Chinese brothers (one 3 years old and one 4 years old) continued to use their home language for several months when communicating with anyone in their English-speaking nursery school classroom. For example, when a teacher (T) was working with a small group of children that included the older of the Chinese brothers (G) and an English-speaking boy (M), the following dialogue occurred (G's utterances are printed in upper-case letters and represent English glosses of what was actually spoken in Chinese):

T: Do you know what that is?
M: Egg.
T: This is an egg. An egg. And what do we do with an egg?
M: You crack it. In a bowl.
T: You crack it. In the bowl.
G: WE EAT THAT.
T: Right. And we call this an egg.
G: IF WE DON'T USE A REFRIGERATOR, THERE WILL BE A LITTLE BIRD COMING OUT.
T: Right. That's an egg. (p. 88)

In this case, the teacher responds to G's comments, even though she cannot understand what he has said. Saville-Troike (1987) reports that this sort of exchange occurred most frequently with teachers; successful dilingual discourse was not a common feature of child–child communication.

The younger of the Chinese brothers continued to use dilingual discourse for 4 more months, but he began to include more and more English in his utterances. The older brother, however, entered a period when he did not use either language. When he was asked by a Chinese interviewer why he had stopped using Chinese in the classroom after 2 months of dilingual discourse, he replied that he "knew that they could not understand him, and he realized that they were not going to learn Chinese. He said that since he was learning English, he would use that language instead" (p. 103).

THE NONVERBAL PERIOD

Sooner or later, then, children faced with a social situation in which their home language is not useful will abandon attempts to communicate in their home language with people who do not understand them. In an English-language classroom, this means that the children will enter a period when they do not talk at all. In a bilingual classroom, it means that children will only attempt to talk with those who speak their home language and will no longer try to talk with those who do not. This period has been observed by a number of previous researchers who have termed it the *silent* or *mute period*.

For example, when I conducted a case study of a young Greek boy, Panos, who was brought to the United States when he was 2 years old, his parents told me that he had attended an English-language child care program five mornings a week for 1½ years before he began to use any English at all. Throughout this time period his Greek was developing normally at home, and his teachers reported that he was actively involved in all aspects of the classroom, although he did not use any English. Finally, in the spring of his second year of child care, he began to use some English in the classroom. By the time I visited him at his child care center when he was 4¾ years old, his English, although a bit singsong in intonation, was well advanced, and he was having no difficulties communicating with everyone in the classroom (Tabors, 1982).

In a case study of another young child, Itoh and Hatch (1978) observed a 2½-year-old Japanese child, Takahiro, who was not only silent in his English-language nursery school setting but also chose to be socially isolated. During his first 3 months at the nursery school, he spent most of his time on a tricycle as far away as possible from the other children. Itoh and Hatch called this a *rejection period* for Takahiro.

Hakuta (1978) also observed a young Japanese girl during a mute period. Although he was eager to begin collecting data about her second-language acquisition, it took from October, when she arrived in the United States, until the following April for her to begin to speak English. During the intervening time she was attending kindergarten and playing with neighborhood English-speaking friends, but she was not producing any English.

Finally, in Ervin-Tripp's (1974) study of American children learning French in Geneva, the researcher found that many of the children "said nothing for many months" and that her own children, ages 5 and 6½, "began speaking after six and eight weeks of immersion in the school setting" (p. 115).

This mute or silent period, then, seems to be a consistent feature of many young children's experience in second-language situations. There seems to be an age component to the length of time that children spend in this period: The younger children in the case studies maintained their muteness for lengthier periods than the older children. This difference is investigated further in Chapter 5.

Nonverbal Communication

For all of these children, the realization that they could not communicate with those around them in their home language meant that they stopped *talking*. But this did not necessarily mean that they stopped *communicating*. Except for Takahiro, who isolated himself from his classmates, most of the young children who have been studied in these circumstances found alternative ways of trying to communicate with those around them. I am, therefore, calling this the *nonverbal*, rather than the silent, period, because although children may not produce utterances during this time, most engage in various forms of nonverbal communication with those who do not speak their home language.

I found that the use of nonverbal tactics by the second-language learners in my study was most common in the first few months in the English-language classroom. For example, one day a dispute arose between Ling Ling and Matthew, who were working with a set of plastic straws and stars at one of the tables. As I turned around, Ling Ling mutely appealed to me by turning her face up to me and looking anxious. My interpretation was that Matthew was trying to take something away from her that she wanted to keep. I moved over to their table, explaining to Matthew that there were plenty of straws and stars for everyone. Then I sat down at the table and began to make a figure out of the straws and stars. When Ling Ling had a problem with what she was building, she handed me the pieces. I put them together for her and handed them back. She was pleased with the result and walked her figure over toward me. I asked, "What's that?" but she shrugged her shoulders. When I asked her if she wanted to take the figure apart, she shook her head vigorously "no." Slightly later Ling Ling was playing with the structure I had built and got it caught on her arm. She extended her arm toward me to show me the problem, and I took it off for her. Next she again handed me a straw and a star. I asked, "You want it on there?" and put it together for her. After this she picked up a large number of straws, put them in an empty box, and left the table to go into the playhouse.

In this sequence Ling Ling uses some of the methods of non-verbal communication that were common among the second-language–learning children in the English-language classroom. She uses the expression on her face to tell me that she needs help when Matthew is trying to take something away from her. Several times she hands me something that she wants fixed. She

advances an object toward me, probably as a prompt for a comment from me. In addition, she is able to respond nonverbally when I ask her questions.

I had similar experiences with other children. One day, Leandro and Naoshi were working with Legos and a set of cards with Lego structures illustrated on them. Leandro was building a police car using the card as his guide. At one point he showed me the card and pointed to a black Lego piece on the card. The piece he needed had been used by Naoshi in a fire truck, but the fire truck was now partially disassembled. I showed Naoshi the card and asked him if Leandro could use that piece for his police car. Naoshi immediately removed the piece and gave it to Leandro.

Here Leandro and Naoshi, like Ling Ling, are using a combination of nonverbal techniques to get a task accomplished or to respond to requests. In all of these examples, the nonverbal communication employed by the children allows them to successfully participate in interactions in a way that would not be possible if these techniques were not used. In other words, the use of nonverbal communication makes it possible for second-language–learning children to be communicative even before they can use the verbal forms appropriate for these situations.

Although nonverbal communication can be effective, it can be used in only a limited set of situations. In the nursery school, second-language–learning children used nonverbal behavior most often to accomplish one of the following: 1) attention getting, 2) requesting, 3) protesting, or 4) joking.

Attention Getting   One of the most typical attention getters used by the second-language–learning children in the classroom involved holding up or showing an object to another person. For example, one day Ling Ling was at a table where there were some piles of different color clay and Popsicle sticks. Joanna was sitting at the table working on a poster for the wall. Rebecca and Matthew were also there playing with the clay. Ling Ling picked up a piece of clay and put it on the end of a Popsicle stick. She held it out in front of Joanna. Joanna took it saying, "Oh, for me?" and pretended to eat it. Ling Ling smiled as she watched, having successfully used a nonverbal attention getter to initiate an interaction with Joanna.

Another morning, at circle time, we were singing the song "Wheels on the Bus." Naoshi got up from the circle, got the toy bus from the shelf, and brought it to show to everyone, demonstrating nonverbally that he knew exactly what the song was all about.

Not all nonverbal attempts at attention getting, however, were successful. Frequently, particularly when nonverbal attention getters were used with other children, there was no uptake from the person whose attention was being sought. For example, one day Ling Ling was working at one of the tables on a building project. In order for her to get some more wooden pegs for her project, she had to stand on a chair and reach into the middle of the table. Also in the same container with the pegs were some pieces of paper on which were colored dots. Ling Ling picked up one of these and waved it in front of Jessica. When there was no response, she put it back in the container. Another day, Naoshi was playing at the sand table. He was using a funnel to cover up a dinosaur toy with sand. As he did this, he looked over at Supat, but Supat was busy with his own play. Then Naoshi laughed out loud and pointed to the dinosaur toy that was buried up to its eyes with sand. Again, he looked at Supat, but Supat did not respond.

In each of these instances it is not particularly surprising that the nonverbal effort by the second-language–learning child does not receive a response, as each effort is quite ambiguous in its meaning, and may, indeed, not be interpretable from the other child's point of view.

Requesting   There were many times during the course of the school day when the second-language–learning children needed help with something they were doing or with a problem they were having with another child. Again, as with attention getting, some of the nonverbal techniques that they used in these circumstances were successful and some were not. For example, one day Byong-sun wanted to play at the water table, but he knew he would need a smock. He walked over to the smocks, looking toward Marion, but she was busy with Naoshi. Then he stood near the smocks for a time, touching one of them. Finally, he took the smock off its peg and brought it over to Marion, who obligingly began to help him get organized for play at the water table.

On another occasion Andrew and Supat were sitting at one of the art tables with a pan with cornstarch and water. When I sat down, Andrew said to me, "Look at the cornstarch. It's making a pattern." At this point Ling Ling, who was also at the table, whimpered, looked toward Joanna, and then looked toward me when I asked her if she needed help. She then held up her arms to me so that I could roll up her sleeves so she would not get them wet with the cornstarch mixture.

In each of these instances it is up to the adult in the situation to know what it is that is being requested, because the amount of information that is being provided by the second-language–learning child is extremely minimal.

If the kind of help that a second-language–learning child needs is not available, the child has only two choices: Try to do it without help or forget about it. Both of these strategies were illustrated one day at the water table in the nursery school classroom. First, Byong-sun wanted something from the other end of the water table. He looked at me and then held his hand straight out. I did not respond, so he left his spot and walked around to the other end where Taro was playing. Upon arrival, he reached into the water and retrieved a plastic bottle and returned to his end of the table. In this case, Byong-sun realized that if he wanted the plastic bottle, he was going to have to go get it himself.

But sometimes it is not possible for a child to solve a problem so easily. Playing near Byong-sun at the water table, Leandro picked up a pump. He tried to make it work but without much luck. Looking around for help, he saw Joanna at the next table, but she was busy, so he merely put the pump down and picked up a funnel. In this case, Leandro seems to decide that it would be more trouble than it was worth to let someone else know that he needed help with the pump, so he decided to forget about it.

Protesting   During the course of the day it was also necessary for the second-language–learning children to let other people know that they were not happy with a particular situation. Examples of children looking upset or whimpering in these circumstances have already been discussed. Another technique, protesting, is revealed in the following two examples.

One day Andrew and Taro were playing with the toy cars at one of the tables. Andrew picked up the car that Taro had left on the table. Taro shrieked. Andrew put the car back and left. On another occasion Naoshi and Leandro were playing with Legos. Each boy had a pile of Legos in front of him. At one point Naoshi reached over and touched one of the pieces in Leandro's pile.

Leandro gave a squeak of protest and took Naoshi's hand away from the piece. Naoshi returned to his own pile of Legos.

Each of these examples demonstrates a behavior used by the second-language–learning children to express the fact that they are not happy with a particular situation. In these two cases, the protest is understood and the situation is changed, but, just as with attention getting and requesting, sometimes a protest is not interpretable, and it is difficult for those around to help.

Joking   It was also possible for second-language–learning children to communicate nonverbally by doing funny things that other people would find amusing. For example, one day Byong-sun was inside the playhouse by himself looking out the window at the end near the bench where Taro happened to be. When Taro spotted Byong-sun in the window, he started to giggle. Then they both giggled and laughed at each other. A little later Taro stuck his head in the window. When Byong-sun saw him, he came back to the window, sticking his hand through again and giggling. Then Leandro came to the end of the house and stuck his head out the window. Taro, who was still on the bench, laughed at Leandro, and then stuck his head in the window.

In this sequence, three second-language–learning children develop a joking game that lets them play together without the use of any language. In fact, this kind of activity was so successful that it had a tendency to become a continuing saga with the children and helped them get into contact with each other and other members of the classroom.

Imitating Nonverbal Behavior   Interestingly, nonverbal communication was so pervasive at the beginning of the school year in this classroom—where more than half of the students were from homes where English was not the primary language—that even one English-speaking child seemed to adopt the behavior. During snack one day, Jessica came over to Joanna and started mugging and miming and pointing toward the table where a bowl of grated cheese was located. During this mugging she wrinkled up her face into a grimace/smile, while closing her eyes and gesturing strongly with her arm. Joanna refused to play the game of guessing what Jessica wanted. Rebecca kindly interpreted that Jessica wanted cheese. Joanna explained that there was already cheese on the pizza. Several more times during snack, Jessica mimed a request, but Joanna ignored her, seeming a bit perplexed by the behavior. Later, at lunchtime, Jessica used the same helpless act with me, needing extra encouragement to get her lunch and pull in her chair.

After this one day, however, Jessica ceased producing this kind of behavior, perhaps because it did not receive the kind of deference she had hoped it would. Nonetheless, it seems likely that the exaggerated gesturing and facial expressions were an overdramatized version of behaviors that Jessica had seen around her among the second-language–learning children, behaviors that received, in her mind, special attention from the adults in the classroom.

Trying to get a message across nonverbally is an appropriate early strategy in second-language settings; most young children in these circumstances seem to be able unself-consciously to call this strategy into play when necessary. The limitations of this behavior are obvious, however. If there is not a helpful and perceptive person available to interpret nonverbal cues, the message may not be received at all.

Social Consequences of Nonverbal Communication   As detailed in the portrait of Byong-sun in Chapter 2, there are also social consequences to continuing to use nonverbal behaviors. As long as the second-language–learning children in the nursery school classroom remained predominantly nonverbal, they were treated like infants by the English-speaking children or ignored as if they were invisible. For instance, one child, Taro, remained predominantly nonverbal during the entire year (see Chapter 9 for a case study of Taro). Andrew, who wanted to be everybody's friend, tried everything he could to communicate with Taro. Andrew's activities included kissing Taro, sticking his tongue out at him, flapping his lips at him, spinning himself around in front of him, chasing and wrestling with him, lifting him up from behind, handing play objects to him, tickling him, and pulling the hood up on his sweatshirt. This behavior on Andrew's part seemed most strongly reminiscent of how an older child might play with a much younger baby.

Furthermore, on at least one occasion, Andrew modified his speech as if he were talking to an infant as he helped get Ling Ling ready for lunch. First, he began to talk to her in a very high-pitched voice. He said, "I'll open your lunchbox." Then he discovered that one of the teachers had already helped her and said,

"Oh, it's empty already." Then one of the children pointed out that some of Ling Ling's milk had spilled on the floor. Andrew walked around to check it out, and when Ling Ling looked like she might start to cry, he said, "Me fix," and went to get a paper towel. When Joanna came to see what was wrong, he assured her, "Me wipe it."

In this sequence Andrew shows two types of modifications that adults often use when communicating with very young first-language–learning children: a high-pitched voice and linguistically reduced forms ("me fix" and "me wipe it"). By using these modifications, Andrew shows his sensitivity to Ling Ling's communicative difficulties, adjusting his speech as if he were speaking with a very young child.

An example of how the English-speaking children regarded a slightly older child who was linguistically different occurred at the end of the school year when a new student, Pierre, came into the classroom. Pierre came to the classroom speaking French; he did not know any English. He was extensively ignored by the other children, although he did make attempts to join in the run-and-chase games that were sometimes played in the classroom as these required no verbal ability.

When one of the teachers took a series of slides of the children in the classroom and then showed them during circle time, a routine developed of naming all the children shown in each slide. Whenever a slide was shown that included a picture of Pierre, all of the other children's names were called out, but never Pierre's. This occurred even though his name was used daily in the classroom by the teachers and was, therefore, known to the other children. Because he had not developed enough English to become a social member of the group, Pierre was apparently invisible to the rest of the children.

Obviously, in order to truly join in the classroom activities as social equals, then, second-language–learning children need to begin to start using the new language.

Gathering Data

During the nonverbal period, children not only devise ways of communicating nonverbally but also begin to gather information about the new language that is being spoken around them. This data-gathering operation consists of two strategies: *spectating* and *rehearsing*.

nearness in place *time*

Spectating   Spectating refers to active observations by the second-language–learning children when they are in proximity to English speakers and are focusing on the language that is being used. In the nursery school classroom, these behaviors frequently occurred during joint activities in which second-language learners and English speakers worked or played side by side or were involved in group activities that involved the whole class.

For example, on the morning when Ling Ling had initiated a play sequence with Joanna by using a piece of clay and a Popsicle stick to make an ice cream cone, Joanna extended the play to the other children at the table, Matthew, Leandro, and Rebecca, by taking their Popsicle stick creations and pretending to eat them as well. After that she made a snake from the clay and turned it into a letter S. Then she asked what other letters they could make. Andrew came by and suggested "O for ostrich." During this entire time, Ling Ling was holding her Popsicle stick with a ball of clay on it, *listening* to and *watching* what was going on with the other children and Joanna.

Later, at circle time, all of the children were singing the songs and playing the games together. Leandro, who was new to the classroom at that time, was standing across from me, *watching* my face intently during the songs. He was slow to copy what the other children were doing at first, but began to get involved near the end.

In these instances, Ling Ling and Leandro seem to be concentrating on watching and listening in order to begin to collect data about the new language to which they are being exposed. What sets this spectating behavior apart from simple, noninvolved listening behavior is the intensity with which it was carried out.

Rehearsing   Rehearsing refers to verbalizations by the second-language learners that did not appear to be communicative, but that indicated these children were working on producing English. Much of the rehearsing was done extremely quietly as the children played near English speakers and was, therefore, difficult to hear. Sometimes it was possible, however, to tune in to the rehearsal as it occurred.

For example, one day when Byong-sun and some other children were working with playdough at one of the tables, Joanna came by and remarked, "Look at that nice playdough," and Byong-sun echoed after her, "Playdough." On another occasion at the water table, Andrew said something that contained the phrase "have to . . ." and Byong-sun, who had been watching Andrew intently, mouthed the words "have to." In these instances, Byong-sun is not trying to communicate with Joanna or Andrew; instead, he is rehearsing the sounds that he has just heard by repeating them out loud. Interestingly, in the second example, Byong-sun is combining spectating behavior (i.e., watching Andrew intently) and rehearsing behavior (i.e., repeating something Andrew has just said).

The nature of this rehearsing process has been more extensively revealed in Saville-Troike's (1988) study as she used directional microphones to capture and record the vocalizations of the young second-language learners. Saville-Troike noted that much of this vocalization was done at such a low volume that even those near the children could not hear what they were saying. Apparently, they were not yet ready to go public with their talk this early in the second-language–learning process.

Similar to the previous examples of Byong-sun's behavior, Saville-Troike (1988) found that the second-language–learning children used repetition as part of the rehearsing process; the younger children usually repeated the end of an utterance that they heard near them, but the older children sometimes repeated more extensive phrases. For example, a 4-year-old Chinese boy (S2) was playing with his back to a group of English-speaking children, but he repeated to himself what they were saying:

Child 1:   Pooty.
    S2:   Pooty.
Child 2:   Pooty?
    S2:   Pooty?
Child 3:   Hey, look.
    S2:   Hey, look.
Child 2:   What are you doing?
    S2:   What are you doing? (pp. 578–579)

Saville-Troike (1988) found that the children also had other uses for this type of private speech, including connecting English words with appropriate objects, actions, or situations or incorporating English in dual-language utterances as if explaining the meanings to themselves.

Sometimes, the children just seemed to be playing with the sounds of the new language, as in this example:

S2:   Yucky. Yucky scoop. Scoop scoop yucky scoop. Yucky yucky yuck-yucky. (Saville-Troike, 1988, p. 583)

Furthermore, some of the children used this rehearsal time to begin to construct pattern drills for themselves in their new language. For example, a 5-year-old Japanese boy constructed the following:

I finished.
I have finished.
I am finished.
I'm finished.

and:

I want.
I paper. Paper. Paper.
I want paper. (p. 585)

During this nonverbal period, then, the young second-language learners were beginning to quietly unravel the patterns of the new language in their environment.

Sound Experimentation

Just as babies must develop control over the sounds of their first language, young second-language learners must develop phonological control over their second language as well. As the previous section shows, some of the rehearsing behavior observed by Saville-Troike (1988) included practice with the different sounds of the new language as well as practice with vocabulary and grammar.

It is well known that young children are particularly sensitive to the sounds of language. In fact, the only feature of second-language acquisition that has been shown to be age sensitive is accent. Young children acquiring a second language are likely to attain native-like pronunciation in the new language, whereas older learners may attain fluency in the language but are less likely to have a native-like accent, even after years of contact with the second language (Snow & Hoefnagel-Hohle, 1977).

A colleague and I were made aware of young children's abilities to concentrate on the sounds of a new language when working on a study of a young Korean child learning English in a book-reading situation (Yim, 1984). In this study, I was the English-language model for Young-joo, a 3-year-old girl who had very little contact with English speakers prior to the study. For the project, I met with Young-joo on a weekly basis and read a book with her in English. Most of Young-joo's and my interactions around the book consisted of my naming objects and Young-joo repeating names (e.g., I said, "This is a moose," and Young-joo repeated, "Moose"), or Young-joo answering questions about objects (e.g., I asked, "Who's that?" and Young-joo answered, "Baby bunny"). On occasion, however, Young-joo would insert invented words into her responses. These invented words were not intelligible as English words, but they were not Korean words either. In fact, my colleague, who was a native speaker of Korean and bilingual in English, reported that Young-joo was using sounds and intonation features that are not present in Korean but are present in English. In using these invented sequences, it seemed as if Young-joo was practicing the tune—

the sounds and intonation patterns of English—before learning all the words of the new song.

Saville-Troike (1988) found the same phenomenon with the two Chinese brothers in her study. She reports that these boys

> Focused extensively on the sounds of the second language, and seemed to relate to the kinaesthetics of pronouncing certain words. High-frequency private vocabulary for them included *butter pecan, parking lot, skyscraper,* and *cookie monster.* Both children also demonstrated their attention to sound by creating new words with English phonological structure, including *otraberver, goch, treer,* and *trumble*—impossible sequences in their native Mandarin Chinese. (p. 583)

Other observers have noticed this phenomenon as well. The mother of one of the English-speaking children in the nursery school reported that her daughter had spent the previous summer in a camp situation with many Spanish-speaking children. When she came home from camp, Rebecca would "speak Spanish" for her mother. Her mother reported that although what Rebecca was saying sounded like Spanish, it did not, in fact, consist of any Spanish vocabulary items. Rebecca had begun to acquire the sound and intonation system in Spanish, and perhaps with longer exposure, she would have begun to acquire some vocabulary items as well.

The second-language–learning children in the nursery school classroom also showed a growing understanding of the sounds and intonation of English. In the first few months in the classroom, there are numerous instances of children talking but without saying anything that could be understood. On occasion, these unintelligible utterances might have been home-language use, but, after the few instances reported on previously, I do not believe that the children were using their home language in the classroom. In fact, I believe that these unintelligible utterances may well have been the type of sound experimentation that Young-joo was using in the book-reading study.

At the time that these strings of sounds were being used by the children, they did not have enough English to express the full idea in their new language, so they used what they had. For example, one morning Byong-sun and Naoshi were playing together at the water table. Because these two boys were from different language backgrounds, they would have to speak English in order to understand each other. The interaction proceeded as follows: Byong-sun held out a cup to Naoshi, accompanying this gesture with an utterance that I could not understand. Naoshi looked over and answered Byong-sun with an utterance with a questioning intonation. Byong-sun then made another utterance with something that sounded like *nice* in the middle, but again I could not understand the whole sentence. After this, they continued their play silently.

This "conversation," one would think, would be considered unsatisfactory, because neither of the participants could have understood the other, but it was not my impression that Byong-sun and Naoshi considered this communication unsatisfactory.

On another occasion, when all of the nursery school children were getting ready to go outside to play, a group of children began fooling around near the door. This upset Ling Ling, who came running in to report the children to the teachers. Although what Ling Ling was saying sounded like English, none of the sentences that she was using could be understood in English. Still, it was clear from the situation what her concern was, and it was quickly taken care of.

Early in the second-language–learning process, then, children may be able to use this ability to mimic the sounds of a new language in a variety of ways. At first, they might structure entire sentences that do not, in fact, contain any English words. Later, they might use these sounds in combination with one or two English words or, eventually, fill in missing slots in a mostly English-language sentence.

For example, one day at the water table Ling Ling had been waiting a long time for one of the pumps, both of which were being used by Byong-sun and Naoshi. Finally, I tried to procure a pump for her by making a request of Byong-sun that ended in "please." Byong-sun gestured to Naoshi and uttered an unintelligible phrase that also ended in "please"—the suggestion being, no doubt, "take his."

On another day in the block area, Leandro had carefully constructed a fenced-in area and supplied it with large plastic farm animals. Naoshi, Supat, and Andrew all came rushing into the area to see what Leandro had done, jumping over the fence. This brought a protest from Leandro. "Don't! (unintelligible) my farm!" Naoshi, Supat, and Andrew climbed out of the fenced-in area and left, leaving Leandro alone in the middle of his farm.

Although not all of the words in the sentence were intelligible, it was clear what Leandro's intention was in protecting his property, and it is possible to even imagine the words that Leandro might have been trying to supply: "Get out of my farm!" or "Be careful of my farm!" By filling the missing slot with sound, Leandro was able to develop a lengthier utterance, which certainly got the desired result.

CONCLUSION

During the nonverbal period, although second-language–learning children are not yet speaking the new language that is being used in the environment around them, they are, nevertheless, beginning to collect data about that new language. Although the children use nonverbal means to communicate their needs, they also use spectating and rehearsing techniques to tune into the new language. Once they feel sufficiently comfortable and competent in this new setting, second-language–learning children begin going public with what they have learned.

chapter four

Speaking a Second Language

As the previous chapter illustrates, young children who are faced with a second-language situation sometimes begin by continuing to use the language that they know, even with people who do not understand their language. For these children, it takes a little time before they realize that this new language is different from the one that they know and that at least some of the people who speak this new language do not understand them when they speak their own language. In a bilingual setting, of course, there may be some people who do and some people who do not understand them and that will take time to sort out as well.

In other words, young children must work through a series of revelations: 1) not everyone understands or speaks their language; 2) the people who do not understand and speak their language understand and speak a *different* language; and 3) if they want to communicate with these people, they will need to learn this new and different language.

Having worked through these revelations, most young children enter a phase of data gathering about the new language before beginning to try to use it. But eventually, sometimes after a lengthy nonverbal period, most young children are ready to try out what they have discovered about the new language in communicative situations.

TELEGRAPHIC AND FORMULAIC SPEECH

When young second-language learners begin to use their new language, observers have noted two consistent features: the use of *telegraphic speech* and *formulaic speech.*

Telegraphic Speech

Telegraphic speech refers to the use of a few content words as an entire utterance; this type of speech is also typical of a period of acquisition by very young children learning their first language. Much of the telegraphic speech in the classroom during the first months of my study revolved around the identification and naming of objects in English. An almost ritualized form was used in soliciting and providing this information. The most basic version of this form involved an adult asking a child "What's this/that?" and then, if the answer were not readily available, supplying the noun herself. So, for instance, when Ling Ling imitated Joanna by building a bridge out of playdough one day, I asked her, "What's that?" She apparently did not know the name in English so she shrugged. I then supplied the word for her by saying "Bridge." She repeated "Bridge," then paused and said it again. In this way it was very easy for Ling Ling to connect the label for the object with the object that she had just made.

If the child was able to answer the "What's this/that?" question, then the next step in this process involved an elaboration or extension by the adult, adding new vocabulary to go with what was already known. For instance, when Leandro was playing in the block area, he brought a car over to me and held it up near my face. I said, "What's that?" He answered, "Car." I elaborated for him, "A racing car."

Quite quickly, the children began to answer the question before it was even asked, showing off and confirming what they already knew how to say. For example, one day at snack time Naoshi pointed to a basket full of crackers and told me "Crackers," then indicated which ones he had selected for himself and said "Three," and then showed me his juice and announced "Apple juice." Each time he received a confirmation from me.

Using these strategies, the second-language–learning children in this classroom began to develop a vocabulary of object names in English that they could use in their interactions with the English speakers around them. Other early accomplishments included counting, naming the ABCs, and identifying colors in English, all basic skills that the English-speaking children in the classroom were also working on at the same time.

Formulaic Speech

The use of formulaic speech has also been documented by researchers studying young second-language learners. This strategy, most extensively detailed by Wong Fillmore (1976, 1979), consists of young children using unanalyzed chunks or formulaic phrases in situations in which others have been observed to use them. These formulas often help children to get into play situations and get their ideas across with a minimum of language.

For example, one day at the water table Naoshi and Byong-sun were playing side by side building a structure out of two bottles with a tube running between them. At one point the tube flipped out of one of the bottles, and Naoshi started to help Byong-sun put it back together. But as he lifted one of the bottles, Byong-sun protested "Stop! Stop!" and when Naoshi did not

stop, Byong-sun took the tube out of the bottle himself. Then Naoshi picked up the tube and tried to insert it in the bottle. Byong-sun started to help him, asking "Okay?" When the structure collapsed again, Byong-sun said, "Uh-oh." As they continued their play, Byong-sun called Naoshi's attention to what he was doing by saying, "Hey." And Naoshi replied, "Okay, okay, okay, okay, okay."

In this sequence, two second-language learners must use all of the useful language they have to communicate with each other. Even though the language they have available is very basic, it is obvious that it makes it possible for the two boys to continue to play together and let each other know how the play is going. Even phrases as minimal as "uh-oh" and "okay" give the communicative partner information about how the play is going, information that would not be conveyed by silence.

On another occasion Naoshi and Leandro had a similar conversation while playing with cars in the block area. As Naoshi ran his car down the radiator he called to Leandro, "Lookit this! Lookit this!" Then he made his car fly up into the air and again said, "Lookit this, Leandro." Leandro finally turned to watch what Naoshi was doing and said in turn, "Lookit" as he showed off what *his* flying car could do, adding engine noises ("zhoooom") as well. Then the two boys traded "Lookit this" and "Lookit that" back and forth five times, until Leandro ended the sequence with "Hey!"

Other phrases that were commonly used by the second-language learners early in the acquisition process were *yes, no, hi, bye-bye, excuse me,* and *I don't know.* These high-utility words were extremely helpful in getting the second-language learners in to and out of social situations in the classroom.

In Wong Fillmore's (1979) study of five first- and second-grade children who had recently arrived from Mexico, it was found that these older children were able to memorize even more extensive phrases. She reports,

> All five [of the children in the study] acquired repertoires of expressions which they knew how to use more or less appropriately, and put them to immediate and frequent use. The phrases they learned were those they found most useful—expressions which helped them appear to know what was going on (e.g. *Oh yeah? Hey, what's going on here? So what? No fighting, now.*), to participate in games

and play activities (e.g. *You wanna play? It's my turn. Me first. No fair!*), and to request information, confirmation, and clarification from their friends (e.g. *How you do this? What's happening? Is this one all right? What did you say?* and *I don't understand*.). (p. 211)

The way that children figure out what the meaning of a word or phrase might be and how it might be used became obvious when Leandro acquired the use of the phrase *be careful* over the course of a week. The acquisition process began one day at lunch when Leandro stood up on his chair and I admonished him to "be careful" while motioning him to get down. He immediately repeated the phrase. Later that same day, Matthew and Rebecca had built a tall tower in the block area and Leandro told them to "be careful." A week later, another tower was being built in the block area. This time Byong-sun, Supat, and Leandro were the builders. Having built the tower too high, the whole structure came crashing down. I said, "Be careful." All three boys repeated after me, "Be careful!" Slightly later that same day, Byong-sun built a tall tower and knocked it down on purpose, shrieking happily and falling into the debris. Leandro, who was sitting at a nearby table working on an art project, said "Be careful."

Another interaction shows how Naoshi acquired an even longer phrase when playing with Andrew in the block area. Naoshi was working on a block structure when Andrew came into the area. Andrew came over to the block structure and said to Naoshi, "Hey, I've a good idea." Then as they tried to add blocks to the structure, Andrew said, "Oh, I'm, I'm, oh, I've got some . . . ," and Naoshi said, "I'm a good idea," putting together Andrew's two previous statements into a new phrase. For the rest of the time they played together in the block area, Naoshi prefaced every move with this new phrase, "I'm a good idea," signaling to Andrew that he was an active participant in their mutual play.

Of course, the children were not always right when they guessed about the meaning of a phrase, which sometimes could cause problems. I observed such an incident one day when Byong-sun was on the ladder to the loft and, meaning to invite Andrew to come up and join him, confidently directed, "Shut up!" Andrew looked surprised and then rather hurt and backed down off the ladder instead of continuing his play with Byong-sun. In this case, Byong-sun was taking the chance that a phrase he had often heard in the classroom, which contained the word *up,* would work in this situation; unfortunately, this time he was wrong.

In general, however, the second-language learners were usually quite quick in their acquisition of at least a limited range of telegraphic and formulaic phrases that helped them socially in the classroom, and they were usually right about the situations in which the phrases could be used. At first these phrases were used most often in communication with the adults and the other second-language learners in the classroom, but as the interaction between Andrew and Naoshi illustrates, they also provided the first opportunities for the second-language learners to begin communicating with the English speakers in the classroom.

PRODUCTIVE LANGUAGE USE

Once second-language–learning children acquire a number of vocabulary items and useful phrases, they can begin the process of *productive language use,* which means that they can begin building their own sentences, not just continuing to repeat formulaic phrases or names for people and things. During this process, second-language–learning children must analyze the language being used around them and begin to make guesses about how the language is constructed. Typically, they use everything they already know about their new language, and, not surprisingly, make many mistakes as they work their way through the process of acquiring the more complicated aspects of English.

Some of the earliest productive phrases in the English-language nursery school were ones that had their origin in the building blocks of telegraphic and formulaic language. For instance, the everpresent *lookit* was often combined with the name of an object, as it was one morning when Ling Ling, Rebecca, and Byong-sun were playing with playdough. Having rolled the playdough into a doughnut shape, Byong-sun presented the results to Rebecca saying, "Lookit dunkin doughnut."

By combining all purpose phrases such as *lookit, I do, I want,* and *I got* with nouns, pronouns, and adjectives, it was possible for the children to generate a variety of creatively constructed phrases, as in the following examples:

One day Akemi, Natalie, Andrew, and Ling Ling were playing with Popsicle sticks and clay. Ling Ling held up a stick with a ball of clay on top and said, "*I do a ice cream.*"

I sat down next to Akemi at one of the tables. She said to me, "Heart," pointing to the heart-shaped dough she had created with the cookie cutter. She followed this up with, "Big. *I got a big.*" In fact, the heart shaped cutter was bigger than all of the others.

One day when Leandro was playing "the baby," his "mother," Jessica, went out of the house area, leaving Leandro alone. Leandro complained, "*I want my mommy.* Mommy!"

Byong-sun was sitting at the table where other children were playing with playdough, but he did not have any. When there was a pause in other talk, Byong-sun spoke up, first very quietly, but then in increasingly louder tones: "*I want . . . want a play-dough. I want a playdough. I WANT A PLAYDOUGH!*"

This "frames and slots" approach was typical of the early productive use of constructed phrases by the second-language–learning children and continued to be a consistent feature of their communications for the remainder of the school year.

Another feature of this period, when the children were beginning to use English productively, was demonstrated most often by Naoshi, who enjoyed word play in his new language. One day, when demonstrating his ability to count in English, he apparently found the usual sequence of 21, 22, 23, and so forth too boring and, therefore, varied it by inventing 20-house, 20-car, 20-light, 20-book.

Another example occurred one day when Naoshi and I were looking at some Styrofoam cups that had been filled with soil, planted with bean seeds, marked with children's names, and put in the sun on the windowsill to grow. As he picked up each cup, Naoshi tried to read the name written on the cup. Several cups, however, did not have names. When he got to a cup without a name he showed me the blank cup and I said, "Nobody." The next cup appeared to be unmarked as well. He held it up to me and said, "Nobody." But then he turned it slightly and discovered a

name. He quickly changed his "Nobody" to "Yesbody." In both
of these cases Naoshi is showing his ability to analyze the structure of English words and vary them in a useful or amusing way.

In Wong Fillmore's (1979) study, the researcher noticed that
the children used their longer phrases to begin the process of
comparison that would lead them to an understanding of the
structure of English. For example, one of the children, Nora,
began with the phrase "How you do dese?" Then she began
adding other material to the end of the sentence to get "How you
do dese little tortillas?" and "How you do dese in English?" She
then realized that other verbs besides *do* could be used in this
construction and came up with "How do you make the flower?"
and "How do you gonna make dese?" Next she acquired the
form *how did you* so that she could make a phrase like *"How did
you make it?"* Next Nora began to vary what came after *How did*
or *How do* to get "How did dese work?" and "How do cut it?"
Finally, Nora realized that *how* could be used as a question word
like *what* and *why* and produced phrases such as "How you make
it?" and "How will take off paste?" As Wong Fillmore comments,

> Looking at this data without the time periods specified, we might
> have guessed that the developmental course went the opposite
> direction—from the less well-formed versions to the well-formed
> ones . . . Indeed, this would have been the case if the acquisitional
> procedure had been a gradual sorting out of the rules whereby the
> learner was able to structure the utterances herself. Instead, the
> procedure was one which might be described as "speak now, learn
> later." (1979, p. 215)

It was often possible to observe this acquisition process as
the children in my study adopted and adapted the language that
other speakers were using. For example, during a play situation
with Legos, Leandro neatly piggybacked his usage on another
child's production. As Sally played with the Legos, she said to
me, "I want to make a tower." Leandro immediately said, "I want
to make this," showing me the card with the police car, substitut-
ing the generic *this* for the noun in Sally's sentence. I said, "Police
car." And he said, "I want to make police." Naoshi asked,
"Police?" And Leandro replied, "Yes, I want to make."

Similarly, on another occasion, Akemi and Matthew were
watching Marion clean out the guinea pig's cage when Matthew
asked, "Marion, can I hold the guinea pig? Can I hold the guinea

pig?" After Marion demurred, "I don't remember making that promise to you," Akemi immediately chimed in, "Marion! Marion! Marion! Can I [have] the guinea pig to hold it, the guinea pig?" And after Marion demurred again, Akemi persisted, "I want a guinea pig, hold a guinea pig." And then when it did not look as if Marion was going to relent, "No-o-o-o, I, I, I, guinea PIG . . . Hold the guinea pig . . . [loudly] I WANT TO HOLD THE GUINEA PIG!" Having demonstrated her language flexibility to its fullest extent, Akemi got the guinea pig to hold.

Leandro was the child who made the most progress in productive language use during his time in the English-language nursery school classroom. Because I was not concentrating on Leandro alone, I do not have an extensive record of the period when Leandro's productive language use in English really began to take form. There are suggestions, however, of how Leandro began to break out of the telegraphic and formulaic forms of usage that he adopted in his early months in the classroom and how he began to develop productive use of English.

Like Nora, there were times when it seemed that Leandro's skills in English were deteriorating. For instance, in December, Leandro, who had always used "I" as the first-person subject of his sentences—but probably in unanalyzed combinations— began to struggle with the I/me distinction that is typical of young children's acquisition of English as a first language.

On December 7, Leandro, who had been at the nursery school for approximately 3 months, was working on a puzzle at one of the tables. As soon as he was finished, Leandro moved away from the puzzle to a spot on the other side of the table where there were rubber pieces that could be put together as a train. He held up a piece and said to me, "Pat. Me make. With my poppy." This comment by Leandro has the aspect of being a vertical construction, using "me" as the first-person subject of the construction.

One week later, Leandro used both "I" and "me" as first-person pronouns in adjacent utterances when he was playing in the playhouse with Supat. Leandro was languishing in bed with Supat nearby on the floor with a cup and teapot. Leandro said to Supat, "I want a drink. Me sick, me sick." Here the *I want* + noun frame is used for the first statement, but apparently the second statement is being constructed from *me* (referring to self) + adjective. On the same day, Leandro also used the constructions "Me's doctor" (which leads one to wonder if "me sick" might not be "me's sick") and "I'm a friend" (most likely a formulaic phrase).

By January, however, Leandro had resolved this conflict and no longer used "me" as a first-person subject pronoun. On January 30 he told me, "I can see 'cuz I have cat's eyes."

The same kind of pattern can be seen in Leandro's development of negatives. His earliest negatives were formulaic: "Don't do that!" and "No more." Then they got broken down into components:

At circle, Leandro said to Supat (in protest over something Supat had done), *"Don't do that."* Then after a moment's reflection he reversed himself by saying, "Yes, that."

When the police car seemed finished, I said, "Good work." And Leandro replied, *"No more."* But then, after checking the picture one last time, he realized he had missed a piece and said to me, "Yes more" as he pointed to the piece in the picture. "Oh, you're right," I said.

The next step in this process was for Leandro to use "no" as a negative insert into a sentence:

At this point Rebecca brought Leandro some "milk" and some "medicine" in containers from the play kitchen. Leandro reiterated to her, *"You no my mommy."*

By January, Leandro had abandoned the negative insert strategy and was able to produce a fully correct negative sentence:

Then Leandro displayed the wallet to me and said, *"I don't have any money in here."*

In this same period Leandro was also working on questions and past tense. In October he asked me, "Your name is what?" but by January he was able to frame a question to Ling Ling as follows, "What you putting in here?" showing that the "what" placement had been regularized but that the auxiliary verb was still missing. In play with Jessica and Andrew, Leandro, who had been pretending to be sick, hopped out of bed as Jessica approached and fled up the ladder to the loft announcing, "You don't gotted me," demonstrating that he had noticed that English verbs in the past tense are usually constructed by adding -ed, but that he had not noticed that this irregular verb was already in the past tense.

THE DEVELOPMENTAL
SEQUENCE: A CUMULATIVE PROCESS

In presenting the information about young children's acquisition of a second language, the developmental sequence was outlined as consisting of four periods: home-language use, nonverbal period, telegraphic and formulaic use, and, finally, productive use. In discussing each of these periods, examples were presented to illustrate the type of interactions that are typical of these periods. It is important to realize, however, that children learning a second language do not move discretely from one period to the next; in fact, except for home-language use, which is usually eliminated when speaking to those who do not understand it, young children add skills to their repertoire from the next level of language use, but maintain the previous techniques as well. In this way, they can bring a range of communicative possibilities to any situation, giving them the best possible chance of getting their meaning across.

The following transcript excerpts illustrate this point. These excerpts are taken from an audiotape-recorded conversation that Leandro and I had one day in April, after Leandro had been in the English-language nursery school for 7 months. We were building with some blocks that could be put together to make a house. During this conversation Leandro demonstrated the variety of levels of competence that he had developed in English by this time. (In the following transcript —— = unintelligible material, L = Leandro, and P = Author.)

L: I need help.
P: Okay. What do you need help with?
L: To —— to building a house.
P: Gonna build a house? (consulting the booklet that came with the building blocks) Which one you gonna build? Which one?
L: This one. Here.
P: Oh, wow.

In the above sequence, Leandro uses a few basic phrases to get my attention, using contextual cues to get his message across.

L: Now we have to make it apart.
P: You want a whole big house.
L: Yeah.
P: Well, I have to start with a wall.
L: I make them apart.
P: You're making a what?
L: Part.
P: Apart? You're going to *take* them apart. Okay.

In the above sequence, there is a classic miscommunication about the word *apart*, which we manage to recover from using appropriate feedback techniques.

P: Let's see, Leandro. You taking them all apart? Let's get some room here.
L: You know what? I want to do it a bell.
P: A . . . a bell?
L: Yeah.
P: What do you mean, a bell. You want to do the house with a bell in it? Where? Show me (looking through the brochure together).

L: ———.
P: You want to build it, huh?
L: Yeah.
P: Okay.

In the above sequence, I continue the conversation by reinforcing the use of the term *apart*. Then Leandro uses a formulaic phrase ("You know what?") to initiate another request for how he wants the house to look, but again I do not understand. Finally, I decide he may mean *build* instead of *bell,* and we proceed.

P: Are you getting all the pieces you need?
L: Yeah.
P: How about some windows? Can you get some windows?
L: The door is a square (looking at the brochure).
P: The door is a square?
L: Yeah. (pause while he goes through the pieces) Can't find.
P: There's no . . . oh, come on, there's got to be a door in here somewhere. There are a lot of things in here. Here're some windows.
L: Windows . . . Here (having found a door).
P: There's a door! Good. Now.
L: No, here's a door ———.
P: Uh! We have two doors . . . Now we need lots of pieces, right?

Here Leandro introduces the terms *door* and *square,* uses a negative construction correctly (*"can't find"*), and answers some of my questions appropriately.

P: Let's see if we can get this door here.
L: How?
P: We have to go up to the top here . . . We need the . . . lintel. (pushing pieces around)
L: And what is for that (showing me a piece)?
P: That's for the corners.
L: For the what?
P: Corner. To go around a corner. Oh, look at this nice big long one. I'm looking for something to go on top of my door.
L: Look at one like that, and one like that.
P: Yeah . . . And here's another one. That can be the other side.

In this sequence Leandro initiates a question about a particular piece (getting the sequence of words slightly wrong), and then asks for a clarification about a new vocabulary item (*corner*).

L: You know what?
P: Oh, here's a window.
L: Lot of windows . . .
P: You need a lot of windows?
L: The house has a lot of windows. (pause) I know what, why have windows?
P: Why?
L: 'Cuz to we can see outside.
P: That's true.
L: It's tru-u-u-e.
P: You couldn't see outside if you didn't have a window, right? (pause) Do you think it would be very dark inside, Leandro, without a window? I-it would be dark, wouldn't it?
L: Yeah . . .

In this complicated sequence, Leandro shows off his ability to construct sentences in English. First he starts with "lot of windows" and puts together "The house has a lot of windows." Then, rather than merely making a statement about why houses have windows, he uses his knowledge to construct a rhetorical question ("I know what, why have windows?") and the answer ("'Cuz to we can see outside"). Although neither of these phrases is correctly formed in English, it is possible to see how far Leandro has come in the process of developing ways to communicate these more complex ideas. Interestingly, Leandro's question and answer encourage me to pose several more questions, which seem to be too sophisticated for Leandro to follow, perhaps because he does not understand the vocabulary.

L: I think that window, window . . .
P: Is that one of these windows? One of these corner windows? Let me put it on the corner, huh?
L: Corner . . .
P: Can you get that one to go the right way?
L: Can you put it?
P: . . . There, you can do it. You just had to get those things lined up. (pause) Good. I think you got it . . .

L: The corner window.
P: Yeah . . .
L: Corner window. I didn't know it was a corner window.

This conversation returns to the vocabulary item *corner* about which Leandro had asked for a clarification earlier. Here I use the word, then Leandro repeats it alone and with the term *window,* ending with a statement about his previous lack of knowledge about this term.

L: And we have to do it like that (pointing to the picture).
P: Really big?
L: Yeah.
P: We'll have the world's biggest house, huh?
L: Like . . . (gesturing with his hands like a roof).
P: You mean with a roof?
L: Yeah . . .
P: Okay. That looks like it's going to be hard.
L: Yes. How we going to put it . . . ?
P: I don't know.
L: I think we're going to do it with windows.
P: Okay. We'll have a solar roof.

This sequence demonstrates the full range of Leandro's communicative skills, from nonverbal use when demonstrating the need for a roof, to construction of a complex sentence such as "I think we're going to do it with windows."

From these excerpts it is possible to see how volatile the language abilities of young second-language learners are. When they have both the vocabulary and the grammatical form under control, they can express themselves in highly sophisticated ways, but when a piece is missing from the puzzle of their knowledge, they have to drop back to techniques that they used in previous stages of their development of the second language. This is what makes conversing with young second-language learners such an adventure, as well as what makes assessment of their language skills a very complicated process (see Chapter 9).

It is also possible to see from these excerpts, however, that by this time Leandro had developed all of the building blocks necessary to continue to develop his second-language ability, acquiring vocabulary items and grammatical forms from the interactions he was able to initiate with the English speakers in the nursery school setting. From his first day in the nursery school in September, Leandro had been working hard at figuring out how to understand and make himself understood in this new language environment and by April he was certainly well on his way.

As mentioned previously, however, Leandro was more advanced in his second-language skills than the other children who entered the nursery school at the same time. Chapter 5 explores the reasons for individual differences in second-language learning in young children.

chapter five

Individual Differences in Second-Language Learning

The previous two chapters establish that the second-language–learning process for young children follows a particular developmental pathway. As in all developmental processes, however, there are definite individual differences in how children approach this developmental pathway, and there are differences in how quickly they proceed along it. This chapter discusses these individual differences and the factors that may be involved in creating these differences.

THE APPLICATION OF COGNITIVE AND SOCIAL STRATEGIES

At the beginning of her study of Spanish-speaking children from Mexico, Wong Fillmore (1979) expected that

> The second language development of the five [children] would be fairly uniform after 9 months of exposure to the new language . . . But the results were quite different. By the end of 3 months of observations, it became quite clear that there would be enormous differences among the five children in what they would achieve

during the study year. In fact, after just 3 months of exposure, one child, Nora, had already learned more—or at least she was producing better-formed and more varied sentences—than two of the others, Juan and Jesus, would be able to manage by the end of the study period. And by the end of the study period, Nora herself was speaking English as well as her friends who came from bilingual homes, and very nearly as well as her English monolingual friends. (p. 207)

In looking for the reasons behind these differences, Wong Fillmore (1979) came to believe that "the individual differences found among the five learners . . . had to do with the way in which cognitive and social factors of language acquisition interact together" (p. 207). Therefore, Wong Fillmore used her data to derive a set of strategies that she believed the children had used in the second-language–learning situation. As she explains, "these strategies are phrased as maxims that the children might have formulated for themselves" (pp. 208–209). The level of proficiency that any individual child achieves in the second-language–learning setting might well be related to how well these strategies are employed by the child. The following are Wong Fillmore's (1979, pp. 209–218) social and cognitive strategies:

Social: Join a group and act as if you understand what's going on, even if you don't.

This strategy is critical as a first step in exposure to a new language. By getting into a group situation in which others are speaking the new language, the second-language–learning child will begin to hear language embedded in that context and relevant to that situation. For example, by joining a group of children about to make soup with a teacher, by finding a spot at the water table next to an English-speaking child, or by helping a group of children build a tall tower of blocks, the second-language–learning child demonstrates that he or she is ready to be part of the social network in the classroom. A child who is reluctant to put this strategy into play will remain isolated from helpful social situations and will have less exposure to the new language.

Cognitive: Assume that what people are saying is directly relevant to the situation at hand or to what they or you are experiencing. Metastrategy: GUESS!

In order to make sense of the new language, the second-language–learning child will need to assume that actions and words are connected. When a teacher is holding an object and talking, the second-language–learning child will need to assume that one of the words being used refers to that object, particularly if one word is repeated or emphasized. If another child uses a gesture or action accompanied by a word or words, the second-language–learning child will need to take a chance and act accordingly, testing the hypothesis that the action and the words are connected. The second-language–learning child who is not prepared to take these risks will take longer to make the necessary connections between the immediate context and the language being used.

Social: Give the impression—with a few well-chosen words— that you can speak the language.
Cognitive: Get some expressions you understand, and start talking.

These strategies show why the development of telegraphic and formulaic phrases is so critical. Socially, it is important that second-language–learning children be able to begin to sound like members of the group in order for them to get further exposure to the language; cognitively, these phrases give the second-language–learning children material to begin the process of deconstruction and reconstruction that will eventually lead to the productive use of the language. Furthermore, by beginning to use phrases in the new language, the second-language–learning child will receive feedback on what does and does not work. The child who does not pick up on the possibilities of using telegraphic and formulaic phrases may remain socially isolated, will have less information about how the new language works, and will have less opportunity to use his or her cognitive processes to unravel the new language.

Cognitive: Look for recurring parts in the formulas you know.
Cognitive: Make the most of what you've got.
Cognitive: Work on big things; save the details for later.

All three of these strategies deal with the process of moving from using formulaic phrases to productive use of the new language. Getting beyond the use of formulaic phrases requires considerable cognitive work on the part of the second-language–learning child. It seems as if the child must understand that there are regularities and commonalities in the phrases that he or she hears, extract them for future use, be willing to try them out, and be relatively unconcerned about being wrong. The second-language–learning child who is willing to take chances and use all of the language resources available at any given time will continue to make progress both in comparing his or her own language output to what is heard and in eliciting language input from others. The child who is less ready to employ these cognitive strategies will require a longer period of time in developing productive control over the new language.

Social: Count on your friends for help.

In Wong Fillmore's (1979) study this primarily meant that the children needed to count on the English-speaking friend who was paired with them for the purposes of the study, but in other contexts this could refer to both adult and child friends. Of course, it is imperative that the friend be a speaker of the new language that the child is trying to learn. In order to develop information about the new language, the second-language–learning child must be in communicative contact with those who speak the language; having a friend who is able to maintain this communication is an important part of the process of breaking through the social isolation that accompanies the second-language–learning situation. In a classroom situation, that friend may be a teacher at first or another child who is particularly tuned in to the social needs of a second-language learner. (See Chapter 6 for suggestions about how to provide this sort of friend for second-language learners in preschool classrooms.) The second-language–learning child who is able to recruit a friend or friends in the second-language–learning situation will be included in the social network and will be exposed to more input in the new language; the second-language–learning child who finds this a difficult social challenge will have a harder time eliciting useful input in the new language, thus slowing down the second-language–learning process.

In order to proceed with rapid second-language learning, children would optimally use these social and cognitive strategies to the fullest extent possible, depending on where they are along the pathway of second language development. But, as we have seen from Wong Fillmore's (1976, 1979) study, as well as from my study in the English-language nursery school classroom, young children progress at very different rates. What underlying factors, then, are involved in determining how available these strategies are to young children in the second-language–learning situation?

UNDERLYING FACTORS

Based on the research on young children learning a second language, there are at least four factors that may determine how available the social and cognitive strategies discussed previously may be to an individual child and, therefore, may strongly influence the progress that a child makes in the second-language–acquisition process. These four factors are motivation, exposure, age, and personality.

Motivation

A young child must want to learn a second language. This decision, to actually take on the process of learning a new language, is one that different children come to at different times and in different ways.

It is known that this is an actual decision for children, because there are some children who decide *not* to learn a second language. For example, in Saville-Troike's (1988) study, there was a 5-year-old Japanese girl who informed a Japanese interviewer that English was too hard so she was not going to speak to people who spoke English. She actually followed through with this plan and did not learn any English during the course of the year-long study.

In the same way, one of the children, Juan, studied by Wong Fillmore (1979) "refused to have anything to do with English-speakers, and would only play silently beside the ones I attempted to pair him with for the purposes of the study" (p. 206). Unlike in the study (Yim, 1984) mentioned previously (see Chapter 3) of a young Korean girl learning English in a book-reading situation, the same process of my reading a book with another second-language child, in this case a 3-year old Korean boy, was a total failure as a second-language–learning situation. Unlike Young-joo, the boy listened politely but made no effort to repeat the English words or phrases I was using.

In all three of these cases, therefore, the children simply refused to play the game of second-language acquisition, at least for a particular time period. And, as long as children are placed in communicative situations in which they can continue to speak their home language or in which they can get by without speaking the second language, they may choose not to undertake the difficult task of learning a second language.

Even in situations in which children eventually do decide to begin the second-language–acquisition process, it is possible that the amount of time they spend in the nonverbal period may be related to how long it takes for them to make the decision to start learning the new language. As mentioned previously, the early period in his nursery school classroom was considered a rejection period for Takahiro, the Japanese child studied by Itoh and Hatch (1978). One explanation for this, they believed, was that he "was attempting to avoid dealing with the second language . . . , hoping it would not be necessary to cope with this new learning task" (p. 78).

Other children, although not cutting themselves off entirely from the second-language situation, find ways of avoiding learning much of the second-language being used around them. In situations in which there are sufficient numbers of children who speak the same first language, some children will continue to associate with their same-language friends, forming social groups on that basis. For example, Meyer (1989) studied a group of Korean girls in an English-speaking nursery school who spent most of their time in class playing with each other. When they sought communication outside their group they were highly selective, most often concentrating on communication with their teachers rather than with their English-speaking peers.

In bilingual classrooms, where a group of children speak the same home language, the children can function by using that language in play situations and with any native-language–speaking adults in the classroom who speak their language. If there are also English-speaking adults in the classroom, the children may develop receptive understanding of English, but they may not feel sufficiently motivated to begin speaking the language themselves.

A final factor in how motivated young children may be to learn a new language might have to do with what their parents tell them about language. Children who are short-term visitors may understand that learning a new language is not a high priority for their family; they may develop enough receptive knowledge to get along in the classroom and, perhaps, a few high-utility phrases to get into play with other children, but they may not advance beyond that level. If families have come to the United States to stay, however, and/or if learning English is given high priority within the family, young children will be exposed to a different attitude and may, therefore, make more of an effort to learn English. (Chapter 8 discusses the kinds of decisions that families face when learning English is a high priority and the ways that teachers can help advise parents for whom this is a concern.)

Young children, then, certainly seem to understand that learning a second language is a cognitively challenging and time-consuming activity. Being exposed to a second language is obviously not enough; wanting to communicate with people who speak that language is crucial if acquisition is to occur. Children who are in a second-language–learning situation have to be sufficiently motivated to start learning a new language.

Exposure

Another factor related to how children approach the second-language–learning process is exposure, both prior exposure to the second language and the quantity of exposure in the second-language–learning environment.

Obviously, if a child arrives in the second-language–learning setting with a prior exposure to the new language, this may affect how quickly he or she might start to use the second language in this new situation.

In the English-language nursery school I studied, a 4-year-old Japanese girl, Akemi, joined the class in January. Although she had not been at the nursery school, Akemi had been in the United States for approximately a year before coming to the classroom and had apparently spent considerable time with English-speaking children in her neighborhood. For this reason, Akemi never went through a nonverbal period in the nursery school, but began to show off her high-utility language skills right from the start. On the first day I observed her, Akemi went into the playhouse, picked up the toy telephone, and said, "I know. How are you? You go. Okay. Okay."

The amount of time spent in contact with the new language is also important in terms of the speed with which a child may acquire the language. At the English-speaking nursery school, parents had the option of enrolling their children in school for two, three, or five mornings a week. Only Leandro, the child who made the most progress among the second-language learners, attended the nursery school 5 days a week. Furthermore, Leandro had two older brothers who were attending public school, and his parents reported that the boys often played together using their new language. Leandro, therefore, could be said to have been in a *high-exposure condition* during the year that he attended the English-language nursery school.

Children are also exposed to different levels of a second language depending on how they spend their time in the second-language setting. If they remove themselves from English speakers and keep mostly to themselves or remain in a group of children who speak the same home language, they will be exposed to less second-language talk than if they solicit interaction from the English speakers in the classroom. In my study, for example, when comparing Ling Ling, Naoshi, and Leandro, I found that Ling Ling talked the least to English speakers, and when she did talk to English speakers, it was mostly with adults. In contrast, Naoshi talked more often than Ling Ling with English speakers, but concentrated mostly on talking with English-speaking children. And Leandro, who spent the most time (of these three children) communicating in English, started with a strategy of talking with the English-speaking adults and then moved on to primarily talking with English-speaking children. At the end of the school year, Leandro had made the most progress in English. Naoshi and Ling Ling had also both made progress, but their achievement was not as great as Leandro's.

Age

Age may also play a distinctive role in how a child approaches the second-language situation. As Chapter 1 discusses, young children are at an advantage in second-language–learning situations because the *cognitive demand* of what they must learn is quite low; they do not have to use language in as sophisticated a way as older children. However, younger children are also at a disadvantage, because their *cognitive capacity* is not as great as that of older children. For this reason, younger children may take longer to move along the developmental pathway than older children.

First, as is seen with the two Chinese brothers in Chapter 3, younger children may persist in the use of their home language for a longer period of time than older children. This may be because it takes younger children longer to figure out that the language they are speaking is not being understood and that it is *another*, completely different language that is being spoken to them.

Second, younger children may also spend a lengthier period in the nonverbal period as well. As mentioned in Chapter 3, there seems to be an inverse relationship between the age of the child and the length of time spent in the nonverbal period. For Panos, who came to the United States from Greece when he was 2 years old, this period lasted for almost 1½ years. For Ervin-Tripp's (1974) children, who were 5 and 6½ years old, the period lasted for only a matter of weeks. Again, it can be assumed that it may take younger children longer than older children to formulate a strategy for breaking out of the nonverbal period.

Third, younger children may also take longer to acquire formulaic phrases, to develop strategies for breaking down phrases into useful pieces, and to create productive phrases in their new language. In Chapter 4, the differences between the phrases being used by the children in my study (who were 3 and 4 years old) and those being used by the children in Wong Fillmore's (1976, 1979) study (who were 5, 6, and 7 years old) are striking: The older children were able to acquire and use much lengthier phrases. All other things being equal, then, this would indicate that older children should move into productive second-language use much more quickly than younger children.

Age, then, may be a critical factor in how quickly a child moves along the developmental pathway of second-language acquisition. Because of their more limited cognitive capacity, it may take younger children longer to mobilize their learning skills and apply them to the challenging cognitive task of learning a second language. This lengthier mobilization period may extend the time a child spends in any or all of the stages of second-language acquisition.

Personality

Personality may also play a part in the way an individual child approaches the second-language–learning situation. Researchers studying young children's second-language acquisition have observed that there seems to be a personality continuum stretching from shy and reserved at one end to outgoing and socially tuned in at the other end. Where an individual child's personality can be located along this continuum may have an impact on how quickly that child learns a second language.

Children who tend to be shy and reserved are more likely to approach the second-language situation with more caution. These are the children who take a long time to go public with their newly acquired language skills, spending their time practicing quietly to themselves before anyone can hear them. Byong-sun certainly fits this profile (see Chapter 3), mouthing other children's words before he began to say them out loud himself. In Saville-Troike's (1988) study, six of the nine children entered a nonverbal period during which five of them used private speech as a means of mobilizing information about the new language. (The sixth child who entered a nonverbal period was the Japanese child mentioned previously in this chapter, who decided not to learn any English.) Saville-Troike characterizes the five children who used private speech as inner directed and more reflective in their general learning style. In Wong Fillmore's (1979) study, she characterizes Juan, the child who did not want to communicate with English speakers, as the "most cautious of all" of the children she studied, who "rarely said anything in English unless he was quite sure of himself" (p. 224).

At the other end of this personality spectrum are the children who approach the second-language–learning situation in a more outgoing and socially oriented fashion. The most detailed example of the use of this style comes from Nora, the child in Wong Fillmore's (1979) study who learned the most English during the study year. Wong Fillmore characterizes Nora as

> Quite uninhibited in her attempts at speaking the new language. After the first 2 months, she was able to get by almost exclusively with English, and from the first she was far more concerned with communication than with form. She used what she knew to say what she needed to say, and she usually made good enough sense. (p. 224)

Although she was the youngest of the children studied by Wong Fillmore (at 5 years 7 months at the beginning of the study), Nora

"experienced spectacular success as a language learner" (p. 221). None of the other children in the study even approached her level of achievement. Wong Fillmore comments,

> Nora was particularly motivated by the desire to be part of the social group that spoke the new language, and thus she sought out the company of the children she wanted to be with. At the other extreme, Juan avoided contact with people who did not speak his language. Thus Nora was in a position to learn the new language where Juan was not. That difference presumably had nothing to do with intellectual or cognitive capacity. It was solely a matter of social preference, and perhaps of social confidence as well. (p. 227)

It is easy to see how more outgoing and socially oriented children would find the second-language setting a particular kind of challenge: If they want to communicate with the children who speak the new language, they have to make every effort to learn the new language as quickly as possible. These risk-taking children often plunge almost fearlessly into communication in the new language, making many mistakes, but getting by nonetheless while receiving a lot of exposure at the same time. Instead of hanging back until they believe they are totally competent, they use whatever words they have and hope for the best, counting on those around them to help in the process of getting the message across.

Of course, most children do not fall at the outer extremes of this personality continuum. For most young children, the process of learning a second language means finding a balance between their social needs and their knowledge of the new language. Juggling the social and cognitive demands of the second-language setting is the hard work that these children do on a daily basis.

Obviously, these four factors—motivation, exposure, age, and personality—may combine in any number of different ways for different children, and they can also be highly interrelated. In my study, Leandro was the child who learned the most during the study year. In Leandro's case, it also happened to be true that he was the oldest of the second-language learners (4 years 2 months in September), that he came to the nursery school every morning, and that he was an outgoing child who made friends easily with both adults and children. This combination of factors, rather than one particular factor, certainly gave Leandro a definite advantage in the second-language–learning situation and can be seen to be the source of his success. We can only guess at how different his level of achievement might have been if one or more of these factors had varied.

CONCLUSION

In both Wong Fillmore's (1976, 1979) study and my study, our objective was to document the process of second-language acquisition among young children. In neither case did the researcher make any attempt at intervention in or manipulation of the second-language–learning process. The variations in the achievement levels of the children at the end of the study periods were, therefore, seen to be the result of the interactions among the strategies and factors that this chapter discusses. The fact that children gained more or less control over their new language in a certain time period was seen to be the end product of a series of natural processes. The implication of this research was: *That is just the way it is.*

From an educator's point of view, however, how quickly a child gains control over a second language may be of more than simply academic interest. Educators of children who will soon be moving into or are already involved in primary school classrooms are certainly under pressure from parents and other educators to help children progress as quickly as possible along the developmental pathway of second-language acquisition. The second part of this book therefore presents information about the role that teachers can play in supporting and facilitating the second-language–learning process in their classrooms, as well as their role in working with parents and assessing young second-language learners' progress.

part two

The Teacher's Role

chapter six

Using Communication and Classroom Organization to Support Second-Language Learning

Preschool educators may encounter a variety of second-language–learning situations in their classrooms, from one child who speaks a language other than English to an entire classroom of children who speak the same or a variety of different languages. And, of course, no matter what the second-language composition of a classroom may be at the beginning of the school year, there may be a very different configuration by the end of the school year. Furthermore, one year may not look anything like the next.

Even so, there are some basic ingredients common to all preschool classroom situations in which there are second-language learners. These commonalities make it possible for preschool educators to plan effective classrooms for second-language–learning children. This chapter presents information concerning what the teacher's role is in communicating with second-language–learning children and their families and in organizing the classroom to support second-language learning.

GATHERING INFORMATION ABOUT THE CULTURAL AND LINGUISTIC BACKGROUNDS OF SECOND-LANGUAGE–LEARNING CHILDREN

One of the first questions on a preschool educator's mind at the beginning of the school year no doubt is, "Who are these children in my class?" Answering this question is complicated enough when there is a match between the cultural and linguistic backgrounds of the teacher and the children; when this is not the case, the task of getting information about the children may be even more complicated.

Following are some rules for preschool educators to use as guidelines when embarking on the process of getting information about children in a preschool education classroom.

Rule #1:   Do not make any assumptions about a child's cultural or linguistic background without getting further information.

This is clearly the starting point for any data-gathering activity and should apply equally to all of the children in a classroom. In the process of collecting information from the families, interesting and helpful characteristics may be discovered, like other languages spoken or countries visited, that would otherwise never be known. It is important to remember that if information is collected formally, in a questionnaire format, it must be collected for *all* of the children in the classroom.

Rule #2:   Decide what information is important to know.

If the primary interest is in collecting cultural and linguistic information, then there are certain categories of information that will be important as children move into the preschool education situation. These categories include 1) basic demographic information, 2) linguistic practices in and outside of the home, and 3) relevant cultural practices.

Basic demographic information includes information about where the child was born; when the child arrived in the area; what the family configuration is (including extended family); what, if any, religious affiliation the child has; and what the other child care arrangements are for the child.

Basic linguistic information includes the language(s) spoken at home, the family members who speak those languages, and the language(s) to which the child has been exposed, including when and where.

Important cultural practices information includes child-rearing beliefs about discipline, toileting behavior, and separation problems; food preferences and feeding practices; and how children are expected to behave toward adults and in group situations. Further information might also be collected about culturally appropriate behaviors that diverge considerably from practices in preschool education classrooms.

Rule #3:   Plan how to get this information.

This type of information can be collected from formal questionnaires, from trips to the library, and/or through informal chats with parents or other cultural representatives. In many situations, there is an intake interview when a family applies for admission to a preschool education program or a home visit is done in the first few weeks of school. In either of these situations, basic demographic and linguistic information could be developed from questions asked at that time. If sitting down with the family to answer questions is not an option, sending home a questionnaire with demographic and linguistic questions is a possibility, but one that does not always yield results. If a questionnaire is sent home without response, it may be necessary to have someone with the appropriate linguistic skills call the family to get the answers over the telephone.

Information on cultural practices may be more difficult to acquire. One good starting point for the preschool educator is the library, where books on individual countries, religions, or linguistic groups might provide some insights and some relevant background information. Books or magazine articles also provide historical information that might be important in understanding why a particular family has recently arrived in the community.

Again, however, it is certainly helpful for a preschool educator to have the option of asking parents about their cultural practices. As one Head Start teacher remarked,

> On the home visit paperwork, we have a form that the office wants anyway. What country are you from? What foods do you eat? Do you celebrate any holidays? But those, they don't get down to the behaviors and the traditions, the taking off the shoes things. For

me, it depends on the parent a lot; if they seem like they're the willing kind, I'll come out and ask them.

The preschool educator may also consider asking the parents to include him or her in a community-wide celebration, which could provide important cultural information as well as let the parents know that the educator values their cultural traditions and is interested in knowing more.

Rule #4:   Think about using a variety of ways to get this information.

Getting information from second-language families can be a challenge. One of the most basic hurdles is, of course, finding an effective way to communicate. Here are some suggestions.

First, face-to-face communication in the second language may be the most difficult for the parents. Face-to-face communication requires quick processing and formulation of a response in real time. This takes a relatively high level of proficiency in a language. It is important to remember that if face-to-face communication is used in a language that is a second language for the parents, the questions may be difficult for them to understand and they may have difficulty putting together their answers. Therefore, if face-to-face communication is used, the same question should be asked more than once using slightly different wording to confirm that consistent answers are being given.

Second, written communications in the parents' second language may give them a chance to read and respond in a way that is less pressured than face-to-face communication. Reading ability in a second language may be stronger than speaking ability. Furthermore, written communications can be shared with other members of the same first-language community who can read and write the second language. Parents with low levels of proficiency may seek out a translator to help complete a questionnaire. For this reason, it is important to remember that a completed questionnaire may not represent the actual language abilities of the parents, but may represent their ability to recruit translation help when needed.

Third, communications that can be arranged in the parents' home language (either oral or written) will likely be the most comfortable for the parents. Many programs have parent liaisons who are bilingual in English and in one of the languages spoken by parents in the program. In this case, both written and oral communications can be translated into the home language, and responses can then be translated for the benefit of staff members who do not speak that home language. If a program does not have access to parent liaisons, it will be necessary to develop relationships with community members who can act as translators. Public schools, churches, community agencies, community newspapers, and even local grocery stores are good places to ask about translation services.

These same community resources may also be a good place to seek out cultural information as well. (See also Williams & De Gaetano, 1985.) Frequently, individuals identify themselves as cultural representatives and make themselves available to discuss the cultural differences that they have noticed between their home culture and the culture in their new community. If one of the parents in a classroom assumes such a role, it can make the teacher's job much easier. As the same Head Start teacher quoted previously told me,

> Like Peilan . . . she's great at answering questions. She has been the lifesaver in this room because . . . in the beginning of the year she didn't understand as much, but now she can translate back and forth between Mandarin and English—and that's just been wonderful.

Figure 1 is a sample questionnaire that can be adapted to use in a variety of situations. Questions can be added or dropped depending on the particular information that is needed. In deciding what information to ask for, the teacher should think about its usefulness in the preschool education context.

COMMUNICATING WITH SECOND-LANGUAGE–LEARNING CHILDREN

By collecting the kind of information that is requested in the sample questionnaire, a teacher would have a better idea of the backgrounds of the children who were coming into or who were already in his or her classroom. But this information would only give the educator a starting point when it came to actually communicating with a child who came to the classroom knowing little or no English. This section discusses ideas about how to

Instructions: Please fill out as much as you can. Do not feel you must answer every question. These questions are meant to make your child's experience in our classroom more enjoyable.

1.   Child's name

2.   Father's name

3.   Father's country of origin

4.   Mother's name

5.   Mother's country of origin

6.   What name do you use for your child?

7.   How did you decide to give your child this name?

8.   Does this name have a particular meaning or translation?

9.   Where was your child born?

10.   Where else has your child lived and when?

11.   How long has your family lived in [name of community]?

12.   What language or languages do you use to talk to your child?
      Father:

      Mother:

13.   Do you speak any other languages?
      Father:

      Mother:

_____
                                                        (continued)

Figure 1.   A sample questionnaire that can be used to collect cultural and linguistic information from parents.

Figure 1.   *(continued)*

14. Who else does your child spend time with besides you? (Please include sisters and brothers, aunts and uncles, cousins, grandparents, family friends, and child care providers.)

Name   Relation to child   Age   Language used with child

_____

_____

_____

_____

_____

_____

15. If English is *not* your home language, please estimate how many English words your child knows (circle one):

less than 10   10 to 50   50 to 100   more than 100

16. Do you belong to a particular religious group?

17. List the food that your child likes to eat:

18. List the food that your child does *not* like to eat:

19. What does your child usually eat with? (circle one)

fingers   chopsticks   fork and spoon

20. How does your child let you know he or she needs to use the toilet?

_____

(continued)

Figure 1.   *(continued)*

Please complete the following sentences.

21.   When my child is with a group of children, I would expect my child to

22.   When my child needs help from an adult, I would expect my child to

23.   If my child is misbehaving in class, I would expect the teacher to

· 24.   If my child is unhappy in class, I would expect the teacher to

25.   The most important thing my child can learn in class this year would be

26.   Is there any other information you would like to give us about your family or your child?

communicate with second-language–learning children in ways that will help them understand and begin to use English.

Starting with What the Children Know

A common practice for the teachers I interviewed was for them to ask parents of children whose home language was not English to provide a few important words in their home language, so that the teachers could do some low-level communicating with the children in the first few weeks in the classroom. Words for *listen, bathroom,* and *eat* were very useful in this early period in the classrooms and helped the teachers and the children feel connected. At the same time, by asking the parents to provide these phrases, teachers also deliver the message that they value the home language and are open to finding out more about how the home language sounds and is used.

Starting Slowly

One of the features of the English-language nursery school classroom that I observed was that the teachers did not make immediate efforts to communicate with the second-language learners beyond a welcoming smile and greeting. In fact, they gave the second-language learners a lot of time to become familiar with the classroom situation before approaching them with questions or directives in English. Several times in the first few weeks of school Marion even referred to Byong-sun in the third person (e.g., "Let's give Byong-sun a chance," "Let's show Byong-sun how to pick this up"), including him by using his name without actually directing her speech to him. This approach established the fact that Byong-sun was being considered part of the group, but that specific responses would not be required of him. By setting up such a *low-demand situation,* the teachers gave the second-language learners time to start the adjustment process in this new cultural and linguistic setting.

In fact, the language that the teachers used around the second-language learners in the first month of school was probably too complicated for them to understand anyway, as only 30% of the teachers' communications involved simplified language. This language use was probably similar to, if not the same as, the way they were addressing all of the children, including the English speakers, in the classroom. After all, in the first few weeks of school, the teachers did not know very much about many of the children in the classroom. So their choice was to use standard "nursery school talk" when addressing any of the children. For the second-language learners, this early exposure probably made it possible for them to begin to at least tune in to the sounds of the new language, even though they probably did not understand what was actually being said.

After the first month, however, the teachers switched to less-complicated language in an attempt to help the children begin to understand English. This reminded me of how adults in American culture speak to infants as though they can comprehend sophisticated speech until the infants are old enough to actually start acquiring receptive abilities, at which time adults begin to simplify their speech by using various forms of "motherese" to get their messages across.

This is not to say, however, that teachers should not be responsive to communicative efforts made by the second-language learners. In fact, the rule in the nursery school seemed to be to always respond even if the message from the child was not understandable. Just like the teacher mentioned previously who engaged in dilingual discourse with the Chinese brothers in

Saville-Troike's (1987) study (see Chapter 3), the adults in the nursery school tried to guess what the topic of the message might be and responded accordingly. For example, one day at the drawing table Poram showed her completed project to Marion and said something to her that was unintelligible (i.e., her utterance sounded like a sentence, but it was not possible to understand what she had said). Marion replied anyway, "Oh, are you making that?"

Buttressing Communication

When the teachers in the nursery school started the process of communicating with the second-language learners in their classroom, they frequently "doubled the message" by using words along with some type of gesture, action, or directed gaze. For example, one morning two Japanese sisters, Kumiko and Kaori, arrived with a paper bag full of vegetables. They approached Rosa, who *pointed to the bag* and asked, "What's in there?" Kumiko opened the bag and showed Rosa what was inside. Rosa said, "How about feeding Ponytails [the guinea pig]?" and she walked to the guinea pig cage, *gesturing for the sisters to follow.* At the guinea pig cage, Kumiko began taking the vegetables out of the bag and handing them to Kaori to put in the cage. Rosa *named each vegetable as it was put in the cage,* "Another carrot, and lettuce."

On another occasion, after watching Leandro wander around the room for a while with a painting he had made, I said to him, "Do you want to put it in your cubby?" He started to go to the cubby area, then he stopped and *touched the paint* on the picture. It was still wet. He *showed me this,* so I said, "Shall I hang it up?" *indicating the line* strung up to dry paintings. He brought the picture to me, I hung it up, and he went to the block area. In this example, Leandro uses nonverbal communication to indicate what the problem is with my first suggestion. My response about hanging the picture on the line is reinforced by indicating the location that I am talking about, because this was a special arrangement for hanging up pictures, and I was not sure that Leandro would understand what I was saying.

One of the teachers I interviewed referred to this as using "body language" to help a second-language–learning child understand. I call this technique *buttressing communication,* because

the additional information delivered by a gesture, an action, or a directed gaze adds another dimension that helps the child tune in to exactly what is being talked about, making it easier to get the message.

Repetition

Another technique that is used successfully when communicating with second-language–learning children involves using *repetition*. Saying the same thing more than once gives a child more than one opportunity to catch on to what is being said. If the repetition involves a single item, it may also provide an opportunity for the child to actually learn the word. For example, one morning at the drawing table the following sequence occurred in rapid succession:

Marion to Jennifer: See how Sook-whan did her *hand?*
   Rosa to Poram: Are you going to cut out your *hand?*
Marion to Jennifer: Look at that *hand,* Myong's right *hand.*
  Marion to Miguel: Do you want to trace your *hand,* too?

Frequently the teachers also emphasized the words as they said them and put them at or near the end of the sentence for better comprehension.

Talking About the Here and Now

One major feature of successful communication with second-language learners is that it is grounded in the *here and now*. Talking about what is right there gives the second-language learner a chance to narrow down the field of what the conversation is about and focus in on a more restricted number of options for response as well. As second-language learners begin to use their productive abilities, the context in which the conversation is held also helps the teacher understand what the child is talking about.

For example, one day outside on the playground, I was sitting on a large rubber tire when Poram came to sit down next to me. Quickly Poram discovered that the tire had writing all around it (Firestone, and so forth). She and I started to name the letters and numbers. Poram had little difficulty with any of the letters except the ones that were upside down because of where we were sitting on the tire. Noticing that there was a problem, Poram gestured to me that the letters were in a strange position. I told her "upside down," and she repeated it. The next time she had the same problem she said, "Upside down." She also stumbled over the number 8. After I told her what it was, Poram was able to identify it correctly later on.

In this example, the fact that we were sharing the same physical space and had reference to the same information on the tire helped to make this a successful communicative experience for both of us, including my being able to provide some missing vocabulary items for Poram.

Expanding and Extending

Once children begin to demonstrate their developing capabilities with their new language, teachers can use communicative opportunities as ways of helping children *expand* and *extend* their language skills. In this technique, it is necessary to start with what a child already knows and work from there. For example, one morning when I sat down at a table where children were working with playdough, Sook-whan held up a round piece of playdough to me and said, "Cookie." I replied, "Is this a chocolate-chip cookie? May I eat it?" Sook-whan nodded and I pretended to eat the cookie. I then told Sook-whan, "That's a good cookie." Later, Sook-whan held up a cube-shape piece of playdough and said, "Chocolate." We followed the same procedure as before as I pretended to eat the piece of chocolate and commented on how good it was. This play routine used Sook-whan's original utterance as a starting point and then developed parallel verbal constructions to extend and expand her language knowledge. This turned out to be successful both as communication and as play.

Upping the Ante

One of the difficult judgment calls that teachers have to make when communicating with second-language learners is when to be more insistent that the children get beyond the nonverbal techniques that they have developed and actually use language to get their point across. In order to push the process along, it is often necessary for a teacher to *up the ante*, insisting on verbal communication, for example, before complying with a request.

This was demonstrated one day when Miguel approached Marion with a suspender that had come loose. The following interaction occurred:

Marion: You're trying to tell me something.
Miguel: (no reply)
Marion: Do you want me to do something?
Miguel: (no reply)
Marion: Do you want me to do something with your suspender? Put it on my nose? (starts to do so)
Miguel: Red. (showing her his pants)
Marion: Yes, red . . . red what?
Miguel: Red pants.
Marion: Do you want me to attach this to your red pants?
Miguel: Yes.
Marion: Okay. I'll do that for you.

I found myself in just this same situation one day with Leandro. As I was leaving the art table Leandro walked by, stopped in front of me, and pointed to his untied shoelace. I said, "What do you need?" He paused for a moment and said, "Please do my shoes." I said enthusiastically, "All right!" letting him know how pleased I was at his linguistic accomplishment.

Fine Tuning

When communicating with second-language–learning children, teachers must always estimate what level of proficiency a child has achieved so that their language can be calibrated to that level.

Of course, this is a very difficult task and many mistakes can be made along the way to successful communication. Fortunately, most communicative situations allow for a process of *fine tuning*, when it is possible to reiterate a message in a form that might be more understandable. Not surprisingly, successful communication with second-language learners requires a lot of fine tuning on the part of teachers.

For example, after lunch one day in early November I found Leandro alone in the block area looking at a book. He had a pair of plastic glasses with him that he had been wearing off and on all day. I picked them up and said, "I like your glasses. Are they yours or do they belong here at school?" This complicated question did not get a reply. Then I said, "Do these come from school?" and Leandro shook his head and said, "House." Then I said, "Are they from Halloween?" And he said, "Yes." Slightly later Leandro spotted a piece of candy in my pocket. He asked, "What's this?" I replied, "Candy," and he repeated, "Candy." I said, "Sally gave it to me." He said, "Halloween?" I answered, "Yes."

By realizing that my first question was perhaps too complicated for Leandro to answer and by rephrasing it to make it simpler, I made it possible for Leandro to understand what I was asking. I then took a chance that he would know the term *Halloween* as there had been a lot of talk about Halloween in the classroom. He not only knew what I was talking about but demonstrated how much he knew by turning the conversation around later and using the term to ask me a question. By fine tuning my initiation I was able to prolong a conversation that turned out to be very successful.

Combining Techniques for Communicating with Second-Language Learners

Although these techniques for communicating with second-language learners have been presented individually, they rarely appear separately from each other. In any attempt to communicate with second-language learners, teachers will combine techniques and keep trying until they find out what will work in any given situation. The transcript of my discussion with Leandro at the end of Chapter 4 shows a variety of these techniques being used simultaneously in my efforts to keep the conversation going.

Furthermore, although these techniques have been presented as relevant for communication with second-language–learning preschoolers, they are, in fact, very similar to techniques used to communicate with first-language learners of a slightly younger age group. Marion, for example, talked about how similar the second-language children were to prelinguistic toddlers:

> When I first started here I had a lot of children who really had no English at all, and then—since I'm comfortable with toddlers, toddler was one of my favorite periods with my own children and the use of preverbal communication—that was sort of the level on which I began things.

Intuitively, Marion discovered that she could use the same communicative techniques with her second-language learners that she had previously used with 18-month to 2½-year-old first-language learners. Teachers who have worked with a younger age group will certainly recognize many of these techniques as being those that are needed to communicate successfully with toddlers. Imported into the second-language–learning preschool classroom, they make it possible for teachers and second-language learners to communicate more quickly and with less frustration right from the beginning.

ORGANIZING THE CLASSROOM FOR SECOND-LANGUAGE LEARNERS

How the classroom is set up can have a major impact on how comfortable and secure a second-language–learning child may feel there. As discussed in the previous chapters, there is a strong social component to a second-language–learning child's adaptation to the classroom. Classroom organization can be used to ensure that adaptation occurs more smoothly and more quickly.

Physical Setup: Providing Safe Havens

In observing second-language–learning children in preschool education classrooms, I have often noticed that they choose to settle down to play in physical settings where manipulatives (like Legos, puzzles, playdough, or small blocks) are available. As the portrait of Byong-sun in Chapter 2 shows, his first choice that morning was to go to the table where the Legos were available and to play there for quite some time either alone or in proximity to another child, whom he ignored. The obvious advantage of these locations is that they provide an activity that a child can pursue without asking for help from anyone else or having to negotiate play with other children. As long as there is a space and some materials available, a child can proceed to play without interference, eventually making a decision about whether to interact with other people.

In setting up a classroom for second-language learners, teachers can make sure that they are providing places in the classroom where second-language learners can feel comfortable, competent, and occupied. These areas, which I think of as *safe havens,* can provide the children with a base of operations from which they can move into the rest of the classroom activities when they are ready.

Classroom Routines: Helping
Children Become Members of the Group

The social aspect of the nursery school classroom that proved most helpful for the second-language learners in my study was the fact that the teachers established a consistent set of *routines* for the children. These routines meant that, with a little observation, the second-language–learning children could pick up cues as to what to do and when, using the English-speaking children as models, even before they could understand the language being used around them. The daily schedule of arrival, free play, cleanup, snack time, outside play, and circle time gave the second-language learners a set of activity structures to acquire (e.g., put jackets in cubby, go to rug, find a place at a table for snack, help put toys away), which immediately allowed them to act like members of the group.

For example, one morning early in the school year, when Marion began to organize a soup-making operation at one of the tables, Sook-whan was standing nearby watching. Marion asked her, "Would you like to help, too, Sook-whan?" Sook-whan nodded her head. Marion then announced, "Okay, there will be five helpers." Sook-whan sat down at the table as Marion named the five helpers, including Sook-whan.

In this example, Sook-whan is addressed by the teacher in a questioning tone that includes her name. This routine is similar in general format to routines that occur again and again in the classroom: The teacher begins to display particular types of materials for a project and invites children to engage in the project. From previous experiences, Sook-whan can guess that Marion has asked if she wishes to join the group. Then when she hears her name and sees the other children start to sit down at the table, Sook-whan does the same, indicating that she understands that she has been included. Even without knowing anything more than her own name, Sook-whan could look like she knew what was being asked of her because the situation was a routine one in the classroom.

Other researchers have observed similar situations with young second-language learners. In their case study of a 5-year-old Taiwanese boy acquiring English in a child care center, Huang and Hatch (1978) found that

> Paul's prompt non-verbal responses to verbal commands were frequently misleading. For example, on his second day at school, when the teacher . . . said, "Paul, would you like to sit there?" he smiled and sat down immediately. (p. 121)

The researchers' speculation was that

> If he responded to any verbal cue at all it would be to "Paul." More likely he saw the other children seating themselves and (the teacher) pointing to the chair as she spoke to him. His response was the expected one and could not be taken as evidence of sentence comprehension. (p. 121)

Because children are so good at using established routines to guess what an appropriate action might be in a given situation, it is only when a child guesses incorrectly that this strategy is fully revealed. One day in the nursery school classroom, Naoshi and Rebecca were sitting side by side working independently with story pieces. I sat down next to Rebecca who was having a difficult time setting up the pieces on the plastic stands. Naoshi, however, had figured out how to set up the pieces and was putting some together. Rebecca said to me, "I want to do what Naoshi did." I answered, "Go ahead." She said, "I don't know how." I said, "Ask Naoshi to help you." Rebecca turned to Naoshi and said, "Can you help me to do that?" He handed her one of the plastic pieces. She asked again, "How do you do it?"

He gave her the plastic bag that still had one extra piece in the bottom.

In this example, Naoshi's best guess is that Rebecca has asked him to provide her with pieces that she cannot reach, a typical request in this situation; not actually understanding what she has said, he still responds with an appropriate, if misguided, action in an attempt to be helpful.

In interviews, both Marion and Rosa pointed to these routines as being an important aspect of the classroom, particularly for the second-language learners. (In the following interaction, P = author and M = Marion.)

P: What kind of patterns do you think you have established with the kids? . . . What helps the kids, particularly the second-language kids?

M: I think, one thing, the structure and rhythm of the day is fairly well set. We do have a definite routine . . . at the beginning particularly we try to be fairly consistent about the routine . . .

P: Does it surprise you . . . how quickly the kids seem to pick up on the routines and fit right in and, on the whole, not be confused and . . .

M: Right, it really does.

P: It surprised me!

Rosa mentioned that in the beginning it was a lot of work to establish the routines in the classroom—she could not just stand back and "let it happen"—but, in the long run, it was worth the effort.

Just how powerful routines can be in helping children become members of a group occasionally becomes apparent when a routine changes without the child being aware of the change. Snow (1983) observed just such an incident in Amsterdam, The Netherlands, where a 5-year-old English girl, Nicola, attended a kindergarten classroom. Nicola seemed to be a fully functioning member of the class:

> She participated in art projects, listened attentively during story reading, executed all the steps to the dance during music class. Her only failure came one day when the teacher announced, while passing out snack, "Today we're going to wait until everyone is back at his seat before we open our milk." Nicola failed to observe

this deviation from the standard routine, since she understood not a single word of Dutch, and she was soundly scolded for having disobeyed. Nicola had done such a good job of acting as if she spoke Dutch that betrayal of her ignorance was treated as obstinacy rather than poor language learning. (pp. 148–149)

Fortunately, most teachers of young children in second-language–learning situations are more sensitive to the possibility of a child not understanding verbal instructions than the teacher was in this situation. But Nicola's reliance on classroom routines as a basis for her activities, particularly in the absence of any understanding of the language being used, is quite typical of preschool-age second-language–learning children.

In setting up a classroom for second-language learners, teachers can capitalize on the helpfulness of routines. Early in the school year it may be desirable to have a strict schedule in order to get children oriented to a set of routine situations. Minimizing confusion and maximizing structure will help the second-language learners tune in to the classroom and feel more secure there sooner. Allowing children to participate in activities in easily understood ways will help them join the social group and be exposed to more language.

Small-Group Activities: Ensuring Inclusion

In the nursery school classroom, the teachers were always careful to include a mix of first- and second-language children in organized small-group activities. Whenever there was an activity underway, like making pizza muffins or soup, teachers would invite groups of children to join the activity, particularly mentioning the names of the second-language–learning children so that they would know they were being included. This inclusionary policy had many benefits:

1. The invitation from the teacher made it possible for the child to join the group without having to negotiate entry.
2. Once included around the table, the child would be in social proximity to the other children, making interactions easier.
3. The child would hear a lot of language relating to the activity that was being pursued.

In setting up a classroom for second-language learners, teachers can use small-group activities as an ideal time to begin to get second-language learners involved. Small-group activities, under a teacher's direction, can help second-language learners begin the transition from more isolated to more coordinated play activities.

Social Support: Getting Help from the English-Speaking Children

In the English-language nursery school classroom, the support that was provided to the second-language–learning children came almost entirely from the adults; the English-speaking children chose to play with English-speaking playmates in the classroom until the second-language–learning children began to communicate in English. This pattern developed, no doubt, because the English-speaking children probably believed that the second-language children's unresponsiveness to their social advances was meant as rejection rather than an inability to understand.

This meant that the second-language–learning children had to wait for months to acquire English-speaking friends and to get involved in activities like sociodramatic play that are heavily dependent on language. Is it possible to get second-language–learning children into contact with English speakers more quickly? And if so, would this enhance the acquisition of the second language for these children?

These questions were the basis for an intervention study by Hirschler (1991, 1994) in a preschool classroom serving 3-, 4-, and 5-year-old Khmer-, Spanish-, and English-speaking children at the Demonstration School of the University of Massachusetts, Lowell. This school is based on a multilingual and multicultural model (Tabors, 1988). In this model, children's preliteracy development in their first language is supported during language periods taught by native-speaking teachers. At other times of the day, however, the children join group activities that are conducted primarily in English. Hirschler believed that the English-speaking children in this classroom could act as valuable language resources for the second-language–learning children, if they could be persuaded to interact effectively with them.

Recognizing that children are capable of modifying their speech to less proficient speakers (Shatz & Gelman, 1977), Hirschler (1991) designed an intervention in which she trained five English-speaking children in a variety of strategies for approaching and sustaining interaction with the second-language learners in the classroom. These strategies were ones that Hirschler developed from a review of the literature on input that has been shown to be most beneficial for second-language learners. They are summarized in Table 1.

In order to introduce these techniques, Hirschler (1991) and an assistant used role playing to model the desired behaviors before the entire group of children and then individually with the five children chosen for the study. All of the strategies were understood by the children and all but recasts were successfully elicited during the training sessions. In order to remind the children of these strategies, each was equipped with a reminder bracelet, and posters were placed in the classroom as well.

Interactional data collected pre- and postintervention indicated that rates of initiations to second-language learners increased from 2.5 to 3 times for four of the five children. Rates of turn taking and utterances per turn also increased, as did language modifications. The overall effect of the training, then, was to increase contact between the English-speaking target children and the second-language learners earlier than would have been the case otherwise.

Table 1.   Strategies for interaction used in training English-speaking children to communicate with second-language learners

- *Initiation:*   Children were taught to approach other children, establish eye contact, and ask the children to play with them or with a particular toy.

- *General linguistic aspects:*   Children were taught to speak slowly with good enunciation.

- *Reinitiation:*   Children were taught to repeat the initiation if it met with nonresponse.

- *Request clarification:*   Children were taught to request clarification of a response by the second-language learner if the response was not understood.

- *Recast/expansion:*   Children were taught to repeat an utterance with slightly different wording when the second-language learner indicated a lack of comprehension through nonresponse, noncontingent response, or other nonverbal signs.

Source: Hirschler (1991).

After the intervention, one particular English-speaking child took on a protective and teaching role with several of the Khmer speakers, consequently greatly increasing her interaction with them. In the following example (Hirschler, 1991), Tiffany is showing Therry some shells on the science table:

Tiffany: O.K. have to smell this. O.K.? That don't smell, does it? Ha! That don't smell. That don't smell.
Therry: (giggles)
Tiffany: Hear the ocean? Hear the ocean? Hear it? Oh, this one is loud! You can hear this one. Can you hear it? Wait, come here. Come here. Want to hear it? Look, hear this. Hear the ocean? (p. 100)

In this example Tiffany is functioning much like a teacher working with a second-language learner, using repetition and talk about the here and now to deliver her message.

By helping the English-speaking children understand that the second-language learners needed help and by providing information about how they might help, Hirschler made it possible for the second-language learners to hear more contextualized language than would have been possible if their only conversational partners were the teachers in the classroom.

In these circumstances, the second-language–learning children did not have to wait until they could begin to produce English in order to be included in social groupings with their English-speaking peers. Hirschler (1991) speculates that "this benign form of social engineering could act as a catalyst to language development" (p. 125) for the second-language learners. She suggests that it would be useful to integrate "into the multicultural classroom, through discussion and group activities, the idea that some children are learning to speak English and there are ways that we can help them" (pp. 125–126).

In setting up a classroom for second-language learners, teachers can point out to English-speaking children that there are children in the classroom who speak a different language, that it will take time for them to begin to speak a new language, and that there are some ways that they can help in this process. Teachers might even ask for volunteer helpers or buddies who could be partnered with second-language learners early in the school year to help reduce their isolation and increase their contacts with English-speaking children. Rather than making the second-language learners feel different (they are already feeling different), this approach can help them feel more connected, while at the same time giving English-speaking children valuable information about how to help other children.

CONCLUSION

The suggestions in this chapter related to classroom organization can be seen as ways of accomplishing a particular objective in a second-language–learning setting termed *lowering the affective filter* (Krashen, 1980). Because the social situation can be so difficult for young second-language–learning children, it is possible for emotional factors to override the language-learning process. By making second-language–learning children more comfortable in the social situation, teachers increase the likelihood that their communicative efforts—and those of the English-speaking children in the classroom—will begin to make sense to the second-language learners. By setting up a classroom environment that helps second-language learners feel secure and competent, teachers make the child's second-language–learning task that much easier.

chapter seven

Using the Curriculum to Facilitate Second-Language Learning

In the English-language nursery school classroom that I studied, there were no overt efforts made to tailor the curriculum to the second-language–learning children. Instead, as discusssed in Chapter 1, the teachers proceeded with a general developmental curriculum that included an activity period, during which children could be involved in free play or in teacher-directed activities; a story time, when the children listened to books read aloud by the teachers; snack and lunchtimes, when children gathered at the individual tables in the room; an outside time, when children climbed on structures, rode tricycles, and played games; and a circle time, when all of the children gathered together with the teachers to sing songs and discuss events of interest. What was evident was that this structure, although fulfilling the developmental needs of the English-speaking children in the classroom, also made it possible for the teachers to incorporate many techniques that helped the second-language learners. This chapter discusses the ways in which the classroom curriculum—particularly in a developmental classroom context—can help second-language learners.

SECOND-LANGUAGE LEARNING
IN A DEVELOPMENTAL CLASSROOM

Many early childhood education classrooms are organized around developmentally appropriate practice principles as outlined by the National Association for the Education of Young Children (NAEYC) (Bredekamp, 1987). What are these practices, and how do they relate to second-language–learning children's experiences in preschool classrooms?

As Genishi, Dyson, and Fassler (1994) recount, developmentally appropriate practices "contrast with highly structured or academic ones, once found mainly in skills-oriented elementary classrooms" (p. 251). They continue:

> In our view the document describes "developmentally appropriate practice" . . . as *holistic* (providing for all areas of children's development: physical, emotional, social and cognitive); *individual-focused* (curriculum grows out of teacher observation and informal assessment of each child); and *developmental-interactionist* (learning is an interactive process that takes into account the child's need to act upon the environment in a wide variety of contexts). Thus recommended practices do not include the teaching of skills through highly structured activities or using means of assessment that rely primarily on standardized testing. (pp. 251–252)

For second-language–learning children, this holistic, individual-focused, and developmental-interactionist framework constitutes an ideal setting for the necessary interactions that help them tune in to and begin to practice their new language. (See Chapter 10 concerning developmentally appropriate practice and cultural sensitivity.) As mentioned in Chapter 1, first-language learning occurs in the context of social interactions within the family. For young second-language learners, a similar context, in which understanding adults can fine tune their language to the children's needs and other children can provide further input, recapitulates the successful environment for first-language acquisition. In both cases, it is the child's interaction with the environment that makes it possible for learning to take place. A preschool classroom environment that does not allow the child the opportunity to interact freely and often with speakers of the second language will mitigate against second-language learning; conversely, a classroom in which children are encouraged to engage in meaningful interactions with helpful others will facilitate second-language learning.

In the following section of this chapter, the activity structure of a developmental classroom is used to discuss the types of facilitative techniques for second-language learning that can be incorporated into the curriculum on a daily basis.

Activity Time

Activity time in a developmental classroom is frequently the time when children are most actively involved in exploring and learning about their environment. In many classrooms, it is during this time that children are engaged in hands-on activities that introduce them to materials, concepts, and vocabulary that help them expand their understanding of the world. In many classrooms, it is also during this time that children are given the opportunity to develop their social skills in interaction with other children around play themes that they develop. In each of these types of activity structures—either teacher directed or child initiated—there are opportunities for language to be used in helpful ways with second-language learners.

Teacher-Directed Activities   An extremely useful technique utilized by teachers when working with young second-language learners is to provide what I call *running commentary,* and what others have called "event casting" or "talking while doing." This takes the form of the teacher explaining his or her actions and the actions of others as an activity unfolds. The advantage of this use of language is that it is directly connected to the objects that are present and the actions that are being performed. This technique can provide children with vocabulary items as well as syntactic structures in English.

For example, one morning Byong-sun was participating in a pizza-making operation with Marion and some of the other children at one of the tables. Marion gave Byong-sun some sauce to put on his pizza muffin. Next she provided the grated cheese and said, "We have to put the cheese on. Would you like to put the cheese on? Andrew put cheese on his. Jessica put cheese on hers. Now you are putting cheese on yours." In this example of running commentary, Marion is combining buttressed communication—talking about the cheese as she is handling it—with repetition. The repetition of the word *cheese* helps it stand out as a particular item among the other sounds that Byong-sun is hearing Marion use. Furthermore, she is providing a mini lesson in pronouns for Byong-sun by only varying the subject (Andrew, Jessica, you) and the matching possessive pronoun (his, hers, yours) in each rendition of the sentence, while keeping all the other elements in the sentence the same.

Child-Initiated Activities   Although the English-speaking children in this classroom were slow to initiate conversations with the second-language learners, they did eventually begin to be helpful communicators when the second-language learners were able to demonstrate some ability in understanding English and using some formulaic phrases. When this happened, the children often spent activity time in free play activities that gave the second-language learners a chance to hear much *context embedded language*—language related to the immediate situation—particularly in the course of sociodramatic play.

For example, one morning in December, Leandro was successfully involved in a long play sequence that he initiated by taking up residence on a small platform area built into the loft and declaring, "Here my bed." First Andrew responded by saying good night, then Jessica gave him a good-night kiss, saying "Good night, sweetheart" before leaving the area. Then Myong arrived on the scene, and Rebecca, who had been playing with a telephone nearby, told her, "Leandro's sick." Myong replied, "I got some medicine." At this point Joanna came by. Seeing Leandro in bed she said, "Good night." He answered, "No, sick!" "Oh, you're sick. Who's the doctor?" Joanna asked. Myong responded, "I'm the doctor," and she went to the dress-up area to find the proper attire for her role, coming back with a long white coat and a white apron. Joanna helped her get the coat on and tied the apron around her waist. As this was going on, Rebecca reassured Leandro by telling him. "The doctor will come soon." Joanna then suggested that Myong might need some paper so she could write down her prescription for Leandro. Myong went off to find paper and a marker. Leandro got out of bed to follow her, but Rebecca told him, "Stay in bed. You're sick. Stay in bed." Leandro climbed back into bed.

Then Myong came back and helped Leandro get arranged in bed. Rebecca said, "He needs a shot." Myong started to give Leandro "an examination" while Rebecca went into the house area to get a shot. When Rebecca came back Myong said to her, "Take the medicine, okay?" and Rebecca said to Myong, "Here's the shot." Then Rebecca said, "He needs a shot right in his tummy," and both girls hovered over Leandro administering the shot. While this was going on, Rebecca commented to Leandro, "You're sick," and Myong commented, "I'm a good doctor."

After giving Leandro the shot, Myong asked Rebecca about what had caused his condition. Myong asked, "How did he get sick?" Rebecca replied, "Someone made him sick and he had to go to the doctor." Myong continued to work on Leandro, declaring "He has the rash." Rebecca, however, announced that Leandro was well, and Myong and Rebecca began a new play sequence about going to the swimming pool, leaving Leandro to languish in his bed, alone.

In this play sequence, words like *doctor, shot, medicine,* and *sick* are repeatedly used in the context of the play, giving Leandro a great deal of exposure to these words. An indication of the effectiveness of this type of play for vocabulary acquisition came after Rebecca and Myong had left Leandro alone. At this point, Leandro got out of the bed and went over to the telephone Rebecca had been using. He picked up the telephone and said, "Hello, doctor! Doctor!" Then he put the telephone down and picked up the coat that Myong had been wearing. He announced, "Me's doctor" as I helped him put on the coat. Although he no longer had an audience (other than me) for this play, it was clear that Leandro was beginning to develop the necessary vocabulary so that he could adopt another role in future play sequences.

Book-Reading Time

One of the most challenging times for teachers with both first- and second-language children in their classrooms may be book reading. Trying to keep all of the children engaged in listening to a book being read aloud, when only some of the members of the group may actually understand what is being read, can be difficult. For this reason, particular attention must be paid to developing a book-reading time that will work for all of the participants. Here are some suggestions for teachers:

1. **Keep it short.** Second-language–learning children cannot be expected to sit for long periods of time listening to mate-

rial that they are not able to comprehend. In order to keep the book-reading time from becoming an endurance contest, teachers should choose books that can be presented in a reasonable amount of time. If the book is long and/or the group attention span is short, teachers should consider purposely stopping part way through and, after eliciting what the children think might happen next, putting the book away to be finished at a later time. This technique will help children develop an anticipation for book reading, will keep them interested, and will help them focus on the story line of the book. When the reading recommences, it will also be an opportunity to recap what happened in the story up until that time, giving children a reason to "stay tuned."

2. **Consider small-group book reading**. When teachers sit down with a book and a small group of children, they can tailor how the book is presented and decide how to respond more carefully to the questions from the group. On some occasions, teachers can choose to have a small group that includes both English-speaking and second-language–learning children in the group. At other times, only English speakers or only second-language learners might be included, so that the presentation can be fine tuned for that particular audience.

3. **Choose books carefully**. Presenting a book to a group of children requires preparation. Different children's books lend themselves to different types of presentations, and teachers should be aware of the possibilities of each book before it is read to the group. Any book that will be used in the classroom should be carefully reviewed for content, vocabulary, length, and special features, including cultural sensitivity.

There are many types of books for young children. Everything from alphabet and naming books to sophisticated renderings of fairy tales are available. The selection of a book should be made with the interests and understanding of the children in mind, as well as the integration of the material with other activities going on in the classroom. Information detailing types of books for preschoolers can be obtained from sources such as *Children and Books* (Sutherland & Arbuthnot, 1991). Local librarians are, of course, also excellent resources for choosing books for particular audiences.

Predictable books are of particular interest for use with second-language learners because they feature highly repetitive and simplified text that makes it easy for second-language learners to become engaged with them. Books like the "Spot" series (Hill, 1980) can provide scaffolded text, making it easy for children to respond to them when they are read aloud.

4. **Talk the story, rather than read it**. If the illustrations and story in a particular book are appealing, but the children being read to are not likely to understand the text, teachers can modify the story by telling a version of it in a way that the children will understand. Of course, with often-read books, some children may know the text by heart and want the "real" version. This would be a good moment to explain that sometimes it is necessary to do things a little differently so everyone in the class can understand the story.

5. **Read books more than once**. Multiple readings of books will help children get more information from them each time they listen to the story. Vocabulary that was not understood the first few times may become more accessible with repeated readings. Each time through the book, different aspects should be highlighted, so the presentation will keep the children's interest high.

6. **Encourage children to "read" to other children**. Once children become familiar with a book, they can then become readers of that book to other children, particularly second-language learners. Again, it is not necessary that they have the text exactly right. What is important is that they can convey their interest, excitement, and understanding of the story to another child. A second-language learner may feel more comfortable asking for clarification or definition from another child than in a larger group with the teacher.

Snack and Lunchtimes

Mealtimes in preschool education classrooms are usually times when teachers are involved in many management activities. Just getting the food onto the table and not the floor takes a lot of work and patience. Snack and lunchtime, however, can also be thought of as important times for adults and children to have conversations that can help second-language learners.

One day in a Head Start classroom (Smith, 1996), a teacher was sitting with children during lunch. The following interaction occurred:

Teacher: Do you know what vegetables these are?
Child: No.
Teacher: What's the green vegetable?
Child: B-b-broccoli.
Teacher: Broccoli. What's the orange vegetable?
Child: Carrots.
Teacher: And what's the white vegetable?
Child: Fish.
Teacher: No.
Child: Flower.
Teacher: Cauliflower.
Child: I said that, but I didn't say cauliflower.
Teacher: That's a long name . . . it's a long name to remember.
Child: I know what that's called—cauliflower.

By taking the time to help this child develop and confirm vocabulary related to the food being eaten, the teacher was able to turn an ordinary event into an opportunity to learn. Although this interaction occurred between a teacher and an English-speaking child, it is the type of interchange that could also be useful for a second-language–learning child as a participant or as a listener.

I observed how conversations among a group of children might also work to help second-language learners. One day at the nursery school, Naoshi, Supat, and Andrew were eating lunch at the same table. As Naoshi poured out his drink for lunch he showed it to me and announced, "Cocoa." Then he turned to Andrew to show him his drink, announcing "Cocoa" again. Then he pointed to Andrew's drink and said, "Cocoa." Andrew replied, "No, this is milk." Then Naoshi pointed to Supat and said, "Cocoa." Andrew said, "No, his is probably apple juice." Then Andrew showed Naoshi his thermos and said, "This is in here milk." Naoshi said, "This is [pause] cocoa!" Then Naoshi said, "Milk cocoa." And Andrew repeated, "Milk cocoa?" As lunch continued Andrew took items out of the paper bag he had brought from home. The bag had ink stamps on it for decoration. Twice Naoshi asked, "What's this?" pointing to an object on the

bag. Andrew told him "spider" and "giraffe." Naoshi had a pile of orange sections in front of him on the table. He began to count them out loud, "One, two, three," and then, pointing to his mouth, he said "Four." Andrew looked over and saw only three sections, so he said, "Three orange pieces." But Supat, who had not said anything up until this point, understood what Naoshi was doing. He told Andrew, "That was four and he ate one." Later Naoshi further refined his orange-section–counting technique (after eating another section) by counting "One, two" on the table, "three" pointing to his mouth, and "four" pointing to his stomach.

In this sequence Andrew and Supat are something of a captive audience for Naoshi, who takes full advantage of their presence to collect data on English vocabulary and grammar, as well as demonstrate his knowledge and conversational skills.

In many preschool classrooms, children's names are taped to chairs, and children find their chairs to sit in for snack and lunch. By placing chairs in particular configurations it is possible for teachers to promote interactions of these sorts at mealtimes by placing sociable English-speaking children with second-language learners, making it easier for second-language learners to get into conversation with English-speaking peers.

Outside Time

Most preschool educators think of outdoor activities as chances for developing gross motor skills and cooperative game playing. Most of the outdoor activities I have observed do not require a great deal of language use, which may well be the reason this time is such an important time for second-language learners. In other words, outside time might well be a time when second-language learners can demonstrate physical competence without being put at a linguistic disadvantage.

Furthermore, outdoor games that have highly routinized rules can give children a participation structure that is obvious and easy to get into. Many large-group games have repetitive linguistic features (e.g., "Duck, Duck, Goose"), which are easy for second-language learners to key into and start using themselves. An effective method for using outdoor games as a time for second-language acquisition would be to partner up second-language learners with English-speaking children and have them work cooperatively throughout a game.

Establishing social and play relationships with other children during outside activites may make it easier for children to develop social and play relationships with these same children inside the classroom as well. Teachers who are alert to the possibilities of partnering up children socially could use outside time as an ideal opportunity for getting English-speaking children and second-language–learning children together.

Circle Time

In many preschool classrooms, circle time is a time when all of the children and adults come together, often sitting down in a big circle on a rug or enclosed area. Various activities occur at circle time. Some of the most common are taking roll and noting who is or is not in class, talking about the day of the week and the weather, talking about the schedule for the day and/or upcoming events, asking the children to make choices for activity time, singing songs, and perhaps doing exercises together. If the classroom curriculum is organized around themes, these themes are often introduced at circle time.

Circle time in a classroom with second-language learners can be organized in a way that will make the time particularly useful for them. First, as in other areas of classroom organization, it is important for teachers to keep to a certain routine during circle

time. By calling the children's names, then talking about the calendar, and then discussing the weather report, teachers can help second-language learners predict the sequence of events and their required response.

Second, teachers should include songs and movements with highly predictable components and should introduce the words of the songs first without music so that the second-language–learning children have an opportunity to catch on more quickly. In addition, giving children many opportunities to return to their favorite songs also reinforces their learning. Frequently, second-language learners will "find their voice" or "go public" for the first time in their new language as they are singing songs during circle time.

Third, the introduction of theme material during circle time should be kept short, simple, and as visual as possible. By being explicit about the vocabulary involved, teachers can also provide second-language learners with the necessary words to participate in the activities around the theme material.

Fourth, children should be allowed to respond to teachers' questions in unison or on a voluntary basis at circle time. By calling on a second-language learner to respond in front of the entire class, teachers may well render even the most confident child speechless. For example, at circle time one rainy morning in

November in the English-language nursery school, Marion called on Naoshi to ask him what might get wet on a rainy day. Naoshi made some motions with his hands (a typical circle time response), so Marion asked the question again, and Joanna tried to help by making raining motions and touching Naoshi's hair asking, "Did your hair get wet?" This time Naoshi shook his head (another typical circle time motion). Marion interpreted this as a negative response to Joanna's question and scaffolded the situation by suggesting *umbrellas* as an answer as she held up an imaginary umbrella. This brought the sequence to a successful conclusion, but what was clear was that Naoshi was not yet ready to respond in this high-demand situation. Letting him offer an answer along with the other children or letting him indicate that he had an answer before calling on him would have made it a much more comfortable situation for Naoshi.

LANGUAGE LEARNING AT THE LANGUAGE ACQUISITION PRESCHOOL

As mentioned previously, most developmental preschool education classrooms have a variety of goals for the children enrolled in them, including social, emotional, physical, and cognitive development. This chapter's discussion thus far has emphasized that a general developmental curriculum offers many opportunities for teachers and other children to help in the second-language–learning process. These suggestions highlight how second-language learning can be accomplished in the context of a developmental classroom, without requiring a restructuring of a classroom curriculum in order to incorporate them.

It is possible to imagine, however, a classroom in which language acquisition is the main goal guiding curriculum planning and classroom activities. In fact, just such a classroom has been developed at the Language Acquisition Preschool (LAP) at the University of Kansas. This school serves typically developing children, children with specific language impairments, and children for whom English is their second language (Bunce, 1995; Rice, 1991; Rice & Wilcox, 1990, 1995). The LAP classroom shares many of the features of other developmental preschools, providing activities that are aimed at the development of social skills and school readiness. What differentiates the LAP classroom from the others is an emphasis on language development throughout the curriculum, the presence of a variety of children with limited language skills but age-appropriate social and intellectual skills, the consistent emphasis on verbal activities, and the encouragement of verbal interactions among the children.

Beginning with the premise that language is learned in socially interactive settings and that children construct their linguistic systems from the language they hear from adults and more capable peers, the creators of LAP have developed the following intervention strategies to facilitate language development.

1. **Provide opportunities for language use and interaction.** First, LAP teachers provide rich and interesting activities. The curriculum is based on an integrated approach in which a specific weekly theme is used to structure many of the activities for the week. For instance, during a week for which the theme is vacations, props for dramatic play, art activities, story time, group time, and music selections all relate to the theme, with options including everything from taking an airplane trip to singing the Mickey Mouse Song (see Bunce & Watkins, 1995). These activities are meant to engage and interest the children and get them involved in interactions related to the activities.

   Second, LAP teachers concentrate on allowing quiet times when they are not talking in order to provide an opportunity for children to initiate conversation about what they find interesting. As Bunce and Watkins (1995) write,

   > A language-facilitating preschool classroom requires teachers and aides who are comfortable being quiet; if adults in the classroom constantly fill up the language "space," there is little incentive or opportunity for children to participate in verbal interchange. Quiet moments in a classroom are not negative. On the contrary, they provide time for reflection and they encourage child initiations. (p. 45)

   Third, the teachers in the LAP classroom arrange the environment so that not all materials are readily accessible, in order to encourage children's efforts at interaction. "In brief, the idea is to provide opportunities for children to learn and practice requesting materials or assistance when they need it" (Bunce & Watkins, 1995, p. 45).

2. **Provide focused stimulation on particular language features.** The teachers in LAP develop plans that include targeted sounds, words, or forms to be used with particular children. These forms are then modeled in comments or statements made during conversations with the children, and the children are encouraged, but are not required, to repeat the models. These forms are usually ones that the children have not yet produced themselves. Furthermore, teachers recast forms that children do use, so as to maintain their meaning, but change their form to another, grammatically altered form. And finally, teachers recast their own utterances, repeating an idea in a different way, in order to provide several structures for children to compare.

3. **Develop routines to help children connect events and language.** Several of the routines used by the teachers at LAP are the same as ones that have been mentioned previously in this chapter under the developmental classroom section. These include establishing familiar daily routines like arrival time, circle time, and snack time so that children can anticipate what will be coming next and prepare themselves to participate, and using event casting (running commentary) to describe their actions or the actions of the children during these events.

One activity, however, in the LAP classroom—sociodramatic play—is handled quite differently. In the classroom I studied and in many classrooms I have visited, sociodramatic play is most often initiated by the children and facilitated by the teachers (i.e., teachers provide materials and often contribute ideas to ongoing play as Joanna did in the sick-in-bed sequence discussed previously, but, on the whole, sociodramatic play is developed by the children themselves). As I noted, however, this means that second-language–learning children are often not included in sociodramatic play until they have been in the classroom for a considerable period of time. In fact, in the English-language nursery school there were *no* observed instances of verbal interactions by the second-language–learning children in the house area during sociodramatic play until December. As Garvey (1977) has pointed out, sociodramatic play imposes particularly high demands on children's linguistic abilities.

In the LAP classroom, the teachers have taken this aspect of the curriculum and made it the centerpiece of their planning, calling it *scripted dramatic play*. As Bunce and Watkins (1995) explain, "Scripted play is a valuable intervention procedure because it provides opportunities for verbal communication within a meaningful context" (p. 48). Rather than merely providing materials, the teachers at LAP initiate the scripted dramatic play by introducing the roles and the props available for the play, as well as giving background information in a discussion or demonstration prior to the play activity. Each day, the teachers introduce a new activity that exposes the children to a variety of information, vocabulary items, and language routines related to each script (see Bunce, 1995, for further information about these techniques and activity guides from LAP). In this fashion, the children in the LAP classroom are exposed to and participate in a particularly rich and supportive language environment.

4. **Stimulate social interaction between children.** In a technique that is the mirror reflection of Hirschler's (1991) training of English-language children to interact with the second-language learners at the Demonstration School (see Chapter 6), LAP teachers help children interact with each other by redirecting their requests for help by suggesting that they seek help from another child. When a child asks a teacher to intervene with another child, the teacher provides the child with a model of how to initiate the interaction, for example by saying, "Ask Shauntaye, 'May I use this truck?'" If a teacher sees that a child is interested in joining an activity but has not made any verbal request to be included, she might suggest, "Ask Larry, 'May I have some playdough?'" In this way children are provided with a model phrase and the necessary vocabulary, and, because the teacher remains nearby to mediate the communication, usually experience a successful start to further social interaction.

As mentioned previously, many of these strategies are, of course, already in common use in other preschool classrooms. At the Language Acquisition Preschool, however, these techniques have been brought to the forefront of the curriculum effort where they provide the framework for daily planning and for interaction between teachers and children. By highlighting the use of these techniques for language facilitation, the teachers at LAP have been able to help children with language impairments make significant progress within the context of the classroom, while providing an optimum environment for typically developing English-speakers as well as second-language–learning children.

FACILITATING SECOND-LANGUAGE LEARNING IN PRESCHOOL CLASSROOMS

The model of the classroom that works best for second-language–learning children that emerges from this chapter and Chapter 6 is one in which the adults in the classroom provide opportunities for children to engage in useful and purposeful language interactions with sensitive interlocutors, both adults and peers. In order to achieve this, teachers should consider providing the following types of opportunities in their classrooms:

1. A routine and consistent organizational structure in which activities happen at regular intervals and in predictable ways
2. A language-rich environment in which teachers use language techniques that help second-language learners understand, and then begin to use, their new language
3. Discussions with, or perhaps training of, English-speaking children in the classroom to help provide socially appropriate language partners for second-language–learning children
4. A variety of organizational and curricular modifications (e.g., small-group inclusion, safe havens, voluntary sharing at circle time, engaging book-reading sessions, cooperative games) that will help second-language–learning children feel more comfortable, included, and competent

By providing an environment that includes these opportunities and by encouraging children to take advantage of these opportunities, preschool educators can help individual second-language–learning children progress through the developmental sequence outlined previously at the rate and in the way that best fits with their social capabilities and cognitive strengths.

chapter eight

Working with Parents
of Second-Language Learners

Involving parents in the education of their young children is a
clear objective of preschool education. Understanding that parents are the *first educators* of their children, preschool educators
must strive to build a partnership with parents so that home and
classroom activities complement and reinforce each other. When
parents speak a different language and come from a different culture, building this partnership may take more time and effort
because of communication difficulties and cultural differences.
This extra effort is well worth it, however, as parents begin to
contribute to teachers' and children's understandings of cultural
differences, and teachers begin to contribute to parents' understandings of the new cultural contexts in which their children are
being placed. The discussion in this chapter focuses on ways to
include parents of second-language–learning children in the
classroom and on the information educators may be called upon
to discuss with parents. The suggestions in this chapter are meant
to help teachers and parents build the type of partnership that will
be the most beneficial for children.

INCLUDING PARENTS IN THE CLASSROOM

Most preschool programs bring parents into the classroom periodically to lend a hand or to demonstrate a specific talent or skill. These roles should be extended to parents of second-language–learning children as well. In other words, rather than restricting parents of second-language learners to the role of cultural interpreters, they should be offered opportunities to become involved in all aspects of the program.

How can this be done? Some suggestions, along with the benefits that might arise from them, follow.

Lending a Hand

Many parents find this the least difficult role to assume in a classroom. Parents of second-language–learning children can be invited to visit the classroom just to spend time there and see what goes on, and then can be encouraged to help out in a variety of ways from pouring juice to cleaning up the paint area. This type of participation is *low demand* from both a linguistic and a responsibility point of view. During the course of a visit of this kind, parents can get a firsthand look at what goes on in the classroom and can begin to feel more comfortable with the activities that occur there.

Demonstrating a Talent or Skill

Many preschool programs consider parents to be valuable resources to be tapped in a variety of ways to enrich the classroom curriculum. In order to find out what types of talents are available among the parents, teachers might want to consider a questionnaire that would ask all parents about what type of activities they might like to share with the children. This questionnaire could have a few suggestions of successful types of activities that have occurred previously in the classroom, but the activities being solicited should not be restricted. Activities to suggest might include those that the parents enjoyed doing as children themselves and those that they have enjoyed doing with their own child. In this way, a parent will not be limited to demonstrating a stereotypical and perhaps inappropriate cultural artifact, but will be able to present an activity with real personal meaning.

This type of activity is, of course, much more demanding in terms of language and organizational responsibility. In order to

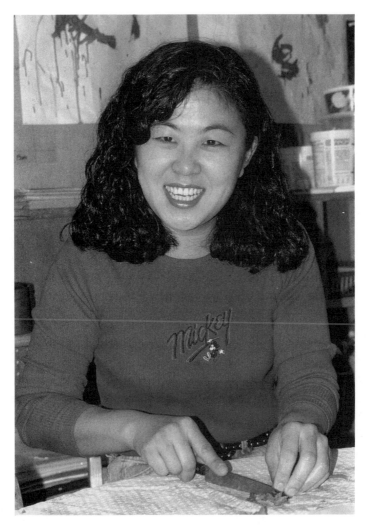

be successful, teachers and parents will have to spend time to-gether planning these activities. For many parents, it might be easier to work with a small group of children at first. As a parent's confidence and comfort level increase, it may be possible to plan activities for the whole group.

Working with Parents Around Cultural Issues

Many teachers believe that it is appropriate to ask parents of sec-ond-language–learning children to come to their classroom to teach some songs in their native language, demonstrate national dress, or develop an ethnic cooking project. If presentations of this sort are made in the context of the overall classroom curriculum, they can certainly be effective in introducing young children to a variety of cultural experiences. For example, in one Head Start classroom that I visited there were many children from China. At the beginning of the school year, three of the children who came to the class had never used forks and spoons. To make them feel more comfortable, the teachers provided chopsticks, and one mother came to the class and helped all of the children learn how to use chopsticks. After the lesson, chopsticks became a permanent feature of the house area, so all of the children could continue to develop their expertise.

If cultural activities are presented in this type of accepting fashion, they can help all of the children feel more comfortable. If cultural activities are presented as strange and exotic, however, they may, in fact, heighten children's feelings of difference rather than commonality. Again, planning and communication before any event will be necessary so that it will be successfully received by all of the children in the classroom.

Maintaining Home-Language Development in the Classroom

Parents of second-language–learning children can also help bring the home languages of the children into the classroom. Rather than restricting parents to the role of translator, teachers should encourage the parents of second-language–learning children to use their home language in meaningful ways when they are in the classroom. This strategy could take the form of the parent presenting an activity using the home language or reading a book to the children in the home language. In this way, the child whose home language is being used in the activity will have the experience of being part of the activity without having to struggle with the language being used; and the children for whom the language being used is not their home language will have the experience of trying to be part of an activity without understanding the language.

Benefits

Some benefits of bringing parents of second-language learners into the classroom are obvious—the parent learns about what goes on in the classroom, and the teacher receives some help. There may be other benefits as well. When a parent of a second-language learner spends time in the classroom, the other children will be able to observe the parent and child talking together, perhaps realizing for the first time that a particular child speaks a different language. If the parent is encouraged to conduct an activity in the home language, the other children will benefit from the experience of being second-language learners themselves.

Furthermore, the presence of the parent of a second-language–learning child may increase the child's social confidence and comfort in the classroom. In the nursery school classroom I observed there was a young girl, Elena, who spoke Russian at home and was very quiet in the classroom. But when her mother came to class one morning, Elena was a different child. She chattered happily with her mother in Russian and participated wholeheartedly in all of the singing and movement activities at circle time. These types of revelations may make it easier for a child to feel more comfortable and find social acceptance in the classroom.

TALKING WITH PARENTS

Most preschool education programs include opportunities for teachers and parents to talk with each other about a child's development and future. These opportunities may range from a quick, informal chat as a child is being dropped off or picked up to a sit-down conference at a prearranged time. The following are examples of questions that parents may ask and the kind of information that educators can use in a conferencing situation no matter where or under what circumstances it is held.

How Is Our Child Doing in Class?

The most basic concern that all parents will have, of course, is that their child is settling into the classroom and participating in the activities being offered there. Teachers will need to be prepared to explain to parents that the process of adjusting to the classroom situation, particularly if there are no other speakers of the child's home language in the classroom, may be slow, requiring patience on the part of the parents and their child. In conferencing with parents of second-language–learning children, therefore, it will be particularly important for the teacher to have in mind developmental milestones that can be emphasized in areas other than language.

Different parents will place different emphasis on the acquisition of English as a primary reason for the child's enrollment in the classroom. Based on questionnaires or conversations with parents, teachers should develop an understanding of the parents' attitudes on this topic and anticipate the types of questions that parents will ask. Understanding the developmental pathway for second-language acquisition discussed in this book will help both parents and teachers gauge an individual child's progress.

One question that parents may have is whether their child is developing friendships with other children in the classroom. As discussed in Chapter 2, social isolation is a common situation for young second-language–learning children in a preschool education setting. The *double bind* that causes this situation—not being able to socialize because they do not know the new language and not being able to develop proficiency in the new language because they cannot socialize—is probably a necessary stage for young children in acquiring a new language in a group setting, so parents will need to be told that this is the case. Parents will, however, also want to know what steps are being taken to reduce their child's isolation and to speed up the process of social acceptance. Having a well-developed plan for including second-language–learning children in classroom activities and being able to articulate that plan to parents will help the teacher allay parental concern in this important area.

Furthermore, teachers can also make a strong recommendation that parents should try to ensure that their children have the opportunity to be in social situations with other children with whom they *do* share a language so that they can continue to develop their social skills in situations in which they are not at a linguistic disadvantage. Parents might be making different decisions on the assumption that they are speeding up the process of language acquisition by keeping their children in all-English situations (see the following section). However, both for maintenance of their home language and development of age-appropriate social skills, it can be critical that young children continue to actively engage in social situations with speakers of their home language.

What Language Should We Be Speaking at Home?

The above question is an extremely important one for many families. Teachers of second-language–learning children will need to understand the dynamics of language acquisition and the circumstances of individual families in order to help parents arrive at a satisfactory answer to this question.

For families that do not intend to remain in the United States, this question does not arise. These parents realize that although their young child may learn some English in a preschool program in the United States, a return to their native country will require maintenance of and continued development in the child's first language. Usually, under these circumstances, families continue to speak their native language at home, sometimes taking on the task of developing the child's preliteracy and literacy skills as well. In these families there may be a need to think about developing some strategies for how they might maintain their child's English proficiency after returning home, but there is never a question that their home language will be supported and maintained by the family. Knowing what families' long-term plans are, therefore, can help teachers evaluate whether or not the question of home-language use will even arise for an individual family.

Families who intend to remain in the United States, however, are faced with a dilemma. For them, the message that comes through loud and clear is, "To be successful in school, your child should learn English as quickly as possible." Many parents believe that the simplest route to fulfilling the promise of this message is to abandon the home language and concentrate on English as the language of choice, even if they have little proficiency in English themselves. But, at the same time, they realize that they will be giving up a great deal in terms of cultural and personal identity along the way. As Panos's father mentioned to me in an interview, "If we end up staying in the States, we would like him to keep . . . a good deal of his Greek . . . We would be happy if we could talk to him in Greek . . . even when he grows up. We feel we communicate better that way . . . We feel that we will be closer" (Tabors, 1982, pp. 10–11). As Wong Fillmore (1991a) has written,

> What is lost when children and families can't communicate easily with one another? What is lost is no less than the means by which parents socialize their children: When parents are unable to talk to their children, they cannot easily convey to them their values, beliefs, understandings, or wisdom about how to cope with their experiences . . . When parents lose the means for socializing and

influencing their children, rifts develop and families lose the intimacy that comes from shared beliefs and understandings. (p. 343)

Abandoning a first language may have extensive personal, familial, religious, and cultural implications. Is it worth the sacrifice? Is this sacrifice necessary?

In order to answer these questions, it is important to go back and examine the first part of the dilemma mentioned previously, the contention that to be successful in school a child should learn English as quickly as possible. In fact, there are good reasons to believe that this is a false premise. What research has shown is that the bilingual children who do best in school are those who have had a strong grounding in their home language, perhaps including development of literacy in that language, before being exposed to a second language (Collier, 1987). Why would this be true?

Much of the cognitive work that children do during the preschool period involves developing concepts about how the world works and learning the vocabulary that helps them express these understandings. Children engage in data gathering about the world by asking questions of adults who are willing to take the time to answer their questions. In this way, children develop an extensive knowledge base about the world that gives them a cognitive framework to apply to the information they will be taught later in school. What is important about these interactions is not what language is used, but what concepts and vocabulary are developed.

As mentioned in Chapter 1, the preschool period is also a time when children are developing discourse skills in their first language. During this period, children begin to use language to put ideas together across a number of utterances. This might be thought of as *speaking in paragraphs.* Helpful adults again play a role in this development, frequently by asking questions, rather than answering them (see Chapter 1). Again, what is important about these interactions is not what language is used, but the extended discourse skills that are developed during the interactions.

What happens if a family decides to abandon the home language and begins to use only English in the home? First, it is unlikely, except in unusual cases, that both parents are equally proficient in English and/or that either of them is as proficient in English as in their home language. Therefore, their interactions with their child will be less rich in vocabulary and less facile in extended discourse in English than they would be in the home language. In other words, not only are parents who are second-language learners themselves rarely good language models for their children, they may also be less well-equipped to help children develop the concepts, vocabulary, and extended discourse skills that are needed in school.

As Richard Rodriguez (1983) wrote about the time after his parents were convinced by the nuns from his school that they should speak English instead of Spanish at home,

> (There) was a new quiet at home. The family's quiet was partly due to the fact that, as we children learned more and more English, we shared fewer and fewer words with our parents. Sentences needed to be spoken slowly when a child addressed his mother or father. (Often the parent wouldn't understand.) The child would need to repeat himself. (Still the parent misunderstood.) The young voice, frustrated, would end by saying, "Never mind"—the subject was closed. Dinners would be noisy with the clinking of knives and forks against dishes. My mother would smile softly between her remarks; my father at the other end of the table would chew and chew at his food, while he stared over the heads of his children. (p. 23)

Convincing parents that there is a benefit to continuing to speak the home language may not be easy for a teacher, as most of the input that parents receive from the popular press, the educational system, and, even, perhaps, within their own cultural group, will point in the direction of switching to English at home as soon as possible. What can teachers tell parents?

One teacher in a workshop mentioned that she tells parents that their role is to teach their children about the world, whereas her role is to teach them the English to talk about what they understand about the world. In this way, she splits the responsibilities for concept formation (to be done at home) and second-language acquisition (to be done at school).

Another teacher, when asked what she tells parents about language, replied,

I've had parents in the past who have said "I want him to go to school and speak English and we're going to start speaking English," and I have to explain to them, you know, don't let them lose their native language, that's *so* important to their self-esteem and, I mean, it's just so important to the family. You know you don't want them to lose that, it could become really valuable. What if he gets older and he needs this job, most people can't speak two languages. This is really important. He might get a job someday over someone else, like me, I can only speak one language, and I tell them only having one language is really hard . . . If I could speak Spanish or Mandarin or Kreyol, I wish I had a second language like that.

If Our Child Does Not Want to Speak Our Home Language, What Should We Do?

As mentioned in Chapter 5, young children often take some time to decide that they are willing to devote the cognitive effort necessary to learn a second language. But by the same token, once they have undertaken that task, they are likely to try to lighten the cognitive load by switching off their first language. This tendency, coupled with a general societal message that English is the preferred language, may lead young children to go from monolingualism in their home language, to active bilingualism (when they are developing both languages), to passive bilingualism (when they stop producing their home language, although they still understand it), and then back to monolingualism, but now in English. Ironically, parents may decide to commit themselves to maintaining their home language, only to have children as young as 4 or 5 years old announce that they will no longer speak the home language and wish to converse only in English.

Wong Fillmore (1991a) writes about a young Chinese girl named Mei-Mei who arrived in the United States from Beijing when she was 3 years old. She and her mother had come to join her father who was already in the United States as a student. Mei-Mei and her mother both began the process of acquiring English as a second language. For Mei-Mei this meant attending an English-language preschool and embarking on the developmental process that has been outlined in this book; for Mei-Mei's mother this meant faithfully attending English as a Second Language (ESL) classes. Predictably enough, after 3 years Mei-Mei had "achieved a native like competence and fluency in the new language" (p. 31), whereas her mother was still struggling with pronunciation and grammar.

At first, Mei-Mei's parents were enthusiastic about using English at home so that Mei-Mei's mother could practice her new language, and Mei-Mei would be ready for school. This plan did not work, however, as Mei-Mei's mother never learned enough English to be able to use it with her. For this reason, the language of the home remained Chinese. However, over the period of a year, Mei-Mei began answering in English when addressed in Chinese, and then began not even understanding what was being said to her in Chinese. When her father asked her to speak Chinese she would say, "Papa, I can't say it in Chinese. Can I say it in English? English is easier."

This course of events, when young children start answering in English when addressed in the home language, then move on to claiming to not even understand the home language, and finally only answering when they are addressed in English, is not uncommon. The problem with this situation is that the child's language development in the home language is truncated, and, just as happens when parents abandon the home language for English, the family loses the sense of intimacy and cultural connection that the home language would otherwise provide. When this happens, parents' concerns turn from, "Will my child ever learn English?" to "How can I keep my child from abandoning our home language?"

Successful home-language maintenance requires that parents be aware that their young children may try to embark on a campaign to stop speaking the home language, and, therefore, must have a counter-campaign in mind.

As mentioned in Chapter 1, Taeschner (1983) was determined to raise her two daughters as German-Italian bilinguals. Her original strategy was to speak German with her daughters, whereas her husband would speak to them in Italian. Taeschner's daughters, however, soon discovered that she also spoke Italian, so they began to speak Italian to her, although they still understood her when she spoke German to them. At this point, her daughters had entered a period of passive bilingualism during which they understood both languages, but would speak only one.

To combat this loss of active bilingualism, Taeschner instituted the following strategy:

> [I] began pretending not to understand most of what they said in Italian. When they spoke to [me] in German, [I] answered immediately and fulfilled their desires. But when they spoke to [me] in Italian, I answered *Wie bitte*? ("What, please?") or *Was hast du gesagt*? ("What did you say?") . . . After awhile, in order to avoid having to say the same thing twice, they began to speak to [me] directly in German. (pp. 200–201)

Even after this strategy proved successful with the girls, Taeschner continued to seek out a variety of ways to keep her daughters interested in German, including trips to Germany, periods of time in German preschools, and the hiring of a German-speaking household helper. Furthermore, she made sure that the children learned to read in both Italian and German, so that their understanding of German could be extended through literacy as well as through personal contact with German speakers. By the time they were 9 years old, both girls were balanced bilinguals who were eager to show off their ability to speak another language with new friends or even casual acquaintances.

There are a variety of recommendations, therefore, that teachers might make to parents. For example, with young children, if the rule has been established that communication must be in the home language at home, then parents might want to institute the practice of not understanding requests made in English. Furthermore, discussions about why it is important to maintain the home language can also prove invaluable with slightly older children. Beyond conversation, reading books written in the home language and watching appropriate television programs or videotapes produced in the home language are other family-oriented activities that can be used to strengthen home-language development.

Just speaking a home language at home, although a good start, may not be enough to allow for the full development of the home language. For this reason, many families make sure that their children have multiple and frequent opportunities to speak the home language outside the home in settings in which there is high communicative demand, such as a preschool or playgroup or extended family, religious, or community gatherings. In these types of circumstances, children learn not only to communicate in different situations with people outside the family, but they also learn the culturally and linguistically appropriate ways to do so. If trips to visit family still living in the areas where the home language is spoken can be arranged, these will also provide high communicative demand situations for young children.

Some families believe it is important for children to acquire literacy in their home language and find that the only way to do this is through an after-school or weekend-school program. In fact, there is a long tradition in many immigrant groups of children attending such schools as a supplement to home-language use. Teachers can endorse parents' use of these schools as a way to continue the development of the home language.

Raising a child bilingually in the United States does not just happen—it requires vigilance and persistence on the part of parents and cooperation and continued practice on the part of the child. Given that there are personal, cultural, cognitive, and even economic reasons to maintain bilingualism, many parents think it is worth the effort.

How Should We Go About
Choosing a School Program for Our Child?

In order to answer the above question, teachers must have considerable information available to them including 1) an assessment of the individual child's skills (see Chapter 9), 2) the family's educational goals, and 3) the school programs available to the child. Teachers should be able to gather the appropriate information about the first two issues within the context of the preschool education setting and in conferences with parents. The third issue, however, will require an information-gathering strategy that goes beyond the confines of the preschool education program.

In order to be able to advise parents of second-language–learning children about what programs are available to them, preschool educators will have to do more than the usual research. Knowing what types of follow-on programs are available for young children has always been part of an effective preschool program, but unraveling the intricacies of programs for second-language learners may offer a further challenge. Knowing what types of programs exist, knowing what questions to ask and what to look for when visiting programs, and knowing how to convey that information to parents will make it easier for teachers to help parents make informed decisions.

Educational programs that serve second-language–learning children, whether public or private, can usually be classified as one of the following: 1) first-language programs, 2) transitional bilingual programs, 3) two-way bilingual programs, 4) general education programs with ESL support, or 5) general education programs with no ESL support. Each of these types of programs, including their defining characteristics, is discussed here.

First-Language Programs   A truly first-language program is a program that is dedicated to the exclusive use of the home language of the children in the program for every interaction in the educational context. As mentioned in Chapter 1, there are researchers and educators who are strong advocates of this approach to education, particularly for young children (Wong Fillmore, 1991b). Historically, immigrant groups were able to establish such school programs, but practice now stresses the development of programs aimed at English-language acquisition with various amounts—from none to a lot—of support for first-language development. For these reasons, it is the unusual community that offers first-language programs except as after-school or weekend options.

Transitional Bilingual Programs   Transitional bilingual education is actually an umbrella term that covers a variety of instructional and programmatic options. In most school systems, transitional bilingual education involves having children who speak the same first language attend class together so that at least part of their instruction each day can take place in their first language. The impetus in most of these programs is, however, to make sure the children leave the bilingual classes as quickly as possible and continue their schooling in general education classes. When evaluating transitional bilingual education programs it is important that teachers keep the following questions in mind:

What are the qualifications of the teachers?
Many bilingual programs cannot keep up with the demand for certified teachers and, therefore, grant waivers in order to fill classroom teaching slots. Just being able to speak a particular language is obviously not a sufficient qualification for being an effective teacher. In some school districts, parents are put in the position of having to choose between a bilingual program in which their children will be taught in their first language by inexperienced teachers or general education programs in which their children's first language will not be supported but the teachers are more proficient.

How is language used throughout the day?
Just as simultaneous bilingual development is most effectively accomplished when young children have one model for each language, children in a bilingual educational context learn best when the languages are not mixed and when translation is not available. Bilingual classrooms should have a clear plan for the use of the two languages in appropriate instructional and conversational situations.

Is the first language maintained? How?
In fact, for young children, this question should really be, "Is the first language being actively *developed*?" A commitment to the development of the first language in the early grades can be found in the reading and language arts instructional program, where the use of the first language would be critical.

How are assessments made concerning children moving into the general education program?
Every school system will have a set of criteria for assessing when a child is ready to leave the transitional bilingual program. Con-

cerns about these assessments and about the timing of bilingual children entering general education programs have been common (Collier, 1989; Cummins, 1984).

How are English-speaking children included in the classroom?
One of the greatest concerns with bilingual education programs is that they segregate second-language–learning children from the English-speaking students. This is troubling for two reasons: 1) a second language is acquired in communicatively demanding situations, and therefore contact with English-speaking peers is vital to the process; and 2) social segregation results in *us versus them* attitudes, and therefore contact with English-speaking peers is critical so that such attitudes, which are so difficult to overcome, will not develop.

Many school systems try to include second-language–learning children with English-speaking peers in such non-academic classes as art and gym, but discover that these efforts are often too little and too late (see Smith & Heckman, 1995). Other systems have adopted more effective plans, for example, by pairing bilingual and general education classrooms with children of same- or different-age levels. When students from both classrooms are together, teachers organize lessons using context-embedded English, sometimes structuring the lessons so that the second-language learners are the "experts," even if their English is not as advanced as the children who are English speaking. Mixing the classrooms as often as once a day for lessons in science or social studies and including plenty of hands-on opportunities and work in small groups helps the bilingual children make gains in English and helps the English-speaking children understand that the second-language–learning children have abilities other than language.

Two-Way Bilingual Programs   A particular type of bilingual program, called *two-way bilingual,* has become increasingly popular (Christian & Whitcher, 1995). These programs match equal numbers of English-speaking children and children from another first-language group and are meant to foster second-language acquisition for each group. In a Spanish-English two-way program, like the Amigos Program in Cambridge, Massachusetts, for example, the Spanish-speaking children learn English and the English-speaking children learn Spanish, and they each have their first language maintained as well.

Even though this type of program has many appealing features, including the social inclusion of the children, the maintenance of the first language, and the development of the second language in a communicatively demanding situation, there are some pitfalls to its adoption as *the* form of bilingual program. First, there must be as many English-speaking parents who want their children to learn the second language as there are second-language–speaking parents who want a two-way program. In practice, what this has meant is that a two-way program will more likely survive if the second language is Spanish than if the second language is Khmer or Punjabi. Second, even if the second language is one that parents have decided is useful for their children to learn, the societal message to their children is the same as the one delivered to second-language–learning children and their parents: English is the important language in the United States. This means that two-way programs are more likely to be successful in promoting English acquisition among second-language–learning children than in promoting second-language acquisition among English-speaking children.

General Education Programs with ESL Support   In school systems in which there are not enough second-language–learning children from a particular language group to require a bilingual program, children often attend general education classrooms with support from an ESL program. In these programs, children who come from a variety of first-language backgrounds are taught English together.

Not surprisingly, ESL programs can be more or less effective depending on how they are structured. The least effective programs are characterized by inappropriate drill and skill approaches to second-language learning with little or no attention to coordination with activities that are occurring in the child's general education classroom. The most effective programs are characterized by developmentally appropriate second-language use included with and/or in support of the curriculum in the child's general education classroom.

No matter how well developed an ESL program is, however, there is not an option within these programs to support first-language acquisition. Parents who wish to maintain their child's home language, therefore, will have to seek other means of doing so.

General Education Programs with No ESL Support   In certain school systems with no previous experience with second-language–learning children, there may be no provision for support for these children. In this case, it will be up to the general education teacher to develop an individual program for the child. An inappropriate approach to this situation is to consign second-language–learning children to the farthest reaches of the classroom until they are "ready to participate." An appropriate individualized program would include many of the techniques of social inclusion and language use discussed in this book for preschool classrooms, but adapted to the primary school setting.

As in the case of general education programs with ESL support, there would be no support for maintenance of the first language in this situation. Again, parents wishing to maintain and develop their children's first language would need to find other ways of doing so.

Summary   From these descriptions it should be clear that labels mean very little in terms of what experience a second-language–learning child may have in any given school system's program. Teachers who wish to be informed about the different programs available to the children leaving their classrooms will need to visit programs, ask questions, and observe in classrooms in order to find out how any program actually works.

Despite this variety of program types and degrees of effectiveness within those types, there are still some basic criteria that should be applied to any follow-on program for second-language–learning children. These criteria are that the program should provide the following:

1. A strong, developmentally appropriate curriculum, including parent involvement
2. Contact with English speakers in a communicatively demanding setting, with social and linguistic support
3. Multicultural understanding and/or support for first language development

If programs with these characteristics do not exist in the community served by the preschool education program, it might well be time for preschool educators to get involved in negotiations with school systems around these issues.

chapter nine

Assessing the Development of Second-Language Learners

Assessing young children's development in meaningful ways is a topic of concern and controversy in the preschool education community. Tests that involve placing a child in a new situation and/or with new people, tests administered only once, and tests that are constructed to display what children do *not* know, rather than what they do know, have all been criticized as being both invalid and unreliable indicators of young children's capabilities. As Meisels (1994) states,

> Measurement in preschool is marked by recurrent practical problems of formulation and administration . . . Many measurement techniques used with older children are inappropriate for use with children below school [age] . . . For example, the following methods are extremely unlikely to yield valid information about normative trends in development: paper and pencil questionnaires, lengthy interviews, abstract questions, fatiguing assessment protocols, extremely novel situations or demands, objectively-scored, multiple choice tests, isolated sources of data. None of these methods are consistent with principles of "developmentally appropriate assessment." (pp. 210–211)

If none of these practices are appropriate for young children in general, their inappropriateness for children from different linguistic and/or cultural backgrounds can certainly be taken as a given (see Genishi & Brainard, 1995). What, then, can teachers do to assess the development of young second-language learners in their classrooms?

GUIDELINES FOR DEVELOPMENTALLY APPROPRIATE ASSESSMENT

There are a variety of assessment techniques that are considered developmentally appropriate for young children. These techniques, which have been growing in popularity among preschool educators, involve the collection of systematic information on a child in the classroom during typical classroom activities by the teacher who works most closely with the child. These are also the types of assessment that are most appropriate for young second-language–learning children.

The National Association for the Education of Young Children (NAEYC) has published the following guidelines related to developmentally appropriate assessment (Bredekamp & Rosegrant, 1995):[1]

1. Curriculum and assessment are integrated throughout the program; assessment is congruent with and relevant to the goals, objectives, and content of the program.
2. Assessment results in benefits to the child, such as needed adjustments in the curriculum or more individualized instruction and improvements in the program.
3. Children's development and learning in all domains—physical, social, emotional, and cognitive—and their dispositions and feelings are informally and routinely assessed by teachers' observing children's activities and interactions, listening to them talk, and using their constructive errors to understand their learning.
4. Assessment provides teachers with useful information to successfully fulfill their responsibilities; to support children's

---

[1]These guidelines are from Bredekamp, S., & Rosegrant, T. (Eds.). (1995). *Reaching potentials: Vol. 2. Transforming early childhood curriculum and assessment.* Washington, DC: National Association for the Education of Young Children; reprinted by permission.

learning and development, to plan for individuals and groups, and to communicate with parents.

5. Assessment involves regular and periodic observation of the child in a wide variety of circumstances that are representative of the child's behavior over time.

6. Assessment relies primarily on procedures that reflect the ongoing life of the classroom and typical activities of the children. Assessment avoids approaches that place children in artificial situations, impede the usual learning and developmental experiences in the classroom, or divert children from their natural learning processes.

7. Assessment relies on demonstrated performance during real, not contrived, activities, for example, real reading and writing activities rather than only skills testing (Engel, 1990; Teale, 1988).

8. Assessment utilizes an array of tools and a variety of processes, including, but not limited to, collections of representative work by children (artwork, stories they write, recordings of their readings), records of systematic observation by teachers, records of conversations and interviews with children, and teachers' summaries of children's progress as individuals and as groups (Chittenden & Courtney, 1989; Goodman, Goodman, & Hood, 1989).

9. Assessment recognizes individual diversity of learning and allows for differences in styles and rates of learning. Assessment takes into consideration children's ability in English, their stage of language acquisition, and whether they have been given the time and opportunity to develop proficiency in their native language as well as in English.

10. Assessment supports children's development and learning; it does *not* threaten children's psychological safety or feelings of self-esteem.

11. Assessment supports parents' relationships with their children and does not undermine parents' confidence in their children's or their own ability, nor does it devalue the language or culture of the family.

12. Assessment demonstrates children's overall strengths and progress, what children *can* do, not just their wrong answers and what they *cannot* do or do not know.

13. Assessment is an essential component of the teacher's role. Since teachers can make maximal use of assessment results, the teacher is the *primary* assessor.

14. Assessment is a collaborative process involving children and teachers, teachers and parents, school and community. Information from parents about each child's experiences at home is used in planning instruction and evaluating children's learning. Information obtained from assessment is shared with parents in language they can understand.

15. Assessment encourages children to participate in self-evaluation.

16. Assessment addresses what children can do independently and what they can demonstrate with assistance, because the latter shows the direction of their growth.

17. Information about each child's growth, development, and learning is systematically collected and recorded at regular intervals. Information such as samples of children's work, descriptions of their performance, and anecdotal records is used for planning instruction and communicating with parents.

18. A regular process exists for periodic information sharing between teachers and parents about children's growth and development and performance. The method of reporting to parents does not rely on letter or numerical grades but rather provides more meaningful, descriptive information in narrative form. (p. 17)

By using these guidelines as a framework, teachers working with young second-language learners will be off to a good start. What is needed beyond these guidelines, however, are some specific strategies for using them effectively with second-language learners that go beyond merely issuing a caution that children's language acquisition and culture need to be taken into consideration. Providing help with these strategies is the goal of the following section.

ASSESSING THE CAPABILITIES OF YOUNG SECOND-LANGUAGE LEARNERS

Teachers working with young second-language learners will need to think about how they will go about assessing those children's capabilities. This process can be divided into three steps: 1) deciding what should be assessed, 2) obtaining assessment information, and 3) using assessment information. This section discusses these three steps in the assessment process for young second-language learners.

Deciding What Should Be Assessed

The first question a teacher must ask when considering the task of assessing a young child is, "What do I want to know about this child?" For a second-language–learning child, the areas of interest might be divided into three categories: 1) the child's capabilities in terms of cognitive, social-emotional, and physical development; 2) the child's capabilities in his or her first language; and 3) the child's capabilities in his or her second language.

The classic division of capabilities for young children into cognitive, social-emotional, and physical development (Goodwin & Goodwin, 1982) is certainly a starting point for assessment of all young children, including second-language learners. For second-language learners, however, difficulties arise quite quickly, as the first two of these areas (cognitive and social-emotional development) as well as perhaps the third (physical development) are extensively involved in and affected by the process of second-language acquisition. In other words, a child's ability to acquire and display information in the cognitive realm may be hampered for a time because of an inability to understand or use the language of the classroom. Furthermore, a child's social-emotional development may be impeded because of a transitory lack of ability in the language used by the other children. Even a child's level of physical development may be difficult to ascertain because of an unwillingness to become involved in games or play. Therefore, teachers must approach assessment in each of these areas with an understanding of the types of constraints that a second-language–learning child is facing. A child's performance in each of these areas must be interpreted with regard to where the child is in the developmental sequence of second-language learning.

Knowing how a child is doing in terms of first-language development can also be crucial in putting together a complete picture of the child's capabilities. For teachers in bilingual settings, this information can be procured in the same way that second-language information is collected. For teachers who do not have access to bilingual resources, however, this important information may remain a missing piece of the puzzle, unless specific steps are taken to procure it.

In addition, teachers will, of course, want to know how a child is progressing in the developmental sequence of second-language acquisition. Even teachers who have an idea of what the milestones are in this developmental process will not have enough information without having strategies for finding out what a child understands and is able to do with the new language.

Obtaining Assessment Information

Knowing what should be assessed is only the first step. Knowing how to go about doing an assessment is the next step.

Assessing Cognitive, Social-Emotional, and Physical Development   The first and strongest caution in terms of assessing a second-language–learning child's overall cognitive, social-emotional, and physical development is for the teacher to give the child sufficient time to adjust to the classroom and to begin to get beyond the linguistic and social constraints of the second-language–learning situation (see Chapter 2) before embarking on any type of assessment except the most informal. In other words, the teacher's careful observation of the child's activities is entirely appropriate, but conclusions based on early observations and placement decisions based on these conclusions can be very misleading and, perhaps, even detrimental to the child's later development.

Furthermore, in assessing a second-language learner's overall cognitive, social-emotional, and physical development, teachers will need to be particularly aware of the abilities that a child can demonstrate *without* the use of language. For example, when a second-language–learning child sits alone at a table and sorts a collection of blocks into different colors, he has demonstrated an understanding of those colors as separate and distinct from each other, even if he is unable to name the individual colors in English. When a second-language–learning child helps another child by filling her juice glass, she has shown an understanding of appropriate social behavior, even though she might not have known what to do if she had been asked. When a second-language–learning child finally does the Hokey-Pokey at circle time after many days of only watching the other children, he has demonstrated a physical capability that was present all along, but that he was only then willing to show off.

With second-language learners it is always necessary to remember that when a child does not respond as expected to any assessment mediated by language, teachers will not know if it is because the child has not developed that capability, has not developed enough language to know what is being asked, or does not have enough language proficiency to respond. For these reasons, teachers will need to develop a series of language-free assessments for cognitive, social-emotional, and physical understandings, and/or will need to be keen observers of children's activities as they occur in order to document what children can and are doing without being asked.

Assessing First-Language Development   Assessing a child's first-language development is crucial to evaluating a child's overall development. If the child's teacher is a proficient speaker of the child's first language, then it may be easy for that teacher to appropriately assess the child's first language in the course of activities in the classroom. If there are few opportunities, however, to speak the child's first language in the classroom or if the child does not feel comfortable displaying first-language capabilities in the classroom situation, then additional steps will need to be taken. Furthermore, if the teacher is not a proficient speaker of the child's first language, it will be necessary to seek other ways of gaining information about the child's language development.

The best place to observe a child's first-language abilities is in the home context. There are many advantages to doing a first-language assessment in the home. The home is where the child is most likely to speak the first language, the child is most likely to feel comfortable speaking the first language, and the people with whom the child speaks this language most often can be found. An informal language assessment can proceed at home in much the way that it would proceed in the classroom. The difference would be, however, that the child can be observed in interaction with parents, grandparents, and/or siblings rather than with the adults and children in the classroom.

Several different methods could be used to obtain information about first-language use during a home visit. First, a bilingual teacher could take notes about the interactions observed in the home, concentrating on whom the child talks to and the level of appropriateness of these interactions. Second, these interactions could be audiotaped with the permission of the parents. In this situation, a teacher who is not bilingual could get help evaluating the audiotapes later by consulting someone who is proficient in the first language. Third, if either of the first two options is not available, the teacher might consider interviewing the parents about their child's first language use, probing for how appropriate they believe their child's language use is in relation to what they would expect. And, fourth, if none of these options are available because of a lack of a common language between the teacher and the parents, the teacher can simply observe the child in communication with family members to see how fluent that communication is, even if the teacher does not understand the language being used.

One teacher I interviewed mentioned using a combination of these techniques. This teacher (M), who is English speaking, told me (P) about how she evaluated a Mandarin-speaking child in her classroom:

M: Actually at the beginning of the year I had some concerns about Kaikai, but then I went to his house and I heard all the talking he was doing in Mandarin. And I was like "He doesn't have a problem. He just hasn't picked up on the English yet."

P: So, one of the things that you have found the home visits useful for is that if you are trying to assess a child's progress in English and not much is going on, you might be worried about whether this is a general problem or whether he's moving into English and this is taking a little bit longer. So going home and seeing how they interact with their parents helps you decide . . . this isn't a big deal.

M: And I also ask the parents. If I think this is a real problem and I don't have a clue, then I ask the parents. And if they say no [it is not a problem], then I don't push the issue.

Assessing Second-Language Development   The final area of assessment that is relevant for young second-language learners is assessment related to their acquisition of the second language. One pioneering effort in developing a system of assessment for bilingual preschoolers is the California Early Language Development Assessment Process (McLaughlin, Blanchard, & Osanai, 1995), which has taken the developmental process outlined in this book as a starting point and has developed both guidelines for assessment of bilingual preschoolers and a detailed process for collecting assessment information.

The guidelines developed for the California Early Language Development Assessment Process are the following:[2]

1.   *Assessment must be developmentally and culturally appropriate.* "In addition to taking into account the social and cognitive aspects of development (Bredekamp, 1987), appropriate assessment for language minority children must take into consideration the unique cultural aspects that affect how children learn and relate to other people" (p. 7).

2.   *The child's bilingual linguistic background must be taken into consideration in any authentic assessment of oral language proficiency.* "Bilingualism is a complex concept and includes individuals with a broad range of speaking, reading, writing,

---

[2]These guidelines are from McLaughlin, B., Blanchard, A., & Osanai, Y. (1995). *Assessing language development in bilingual preschool children.* Washington, DC: George Washington University. (The National Clearinghouse for Bilingual Education, #22, June)

and comprehending abilities in each language. Furthermore, these abilities are constantly in flux" (p. 7).

3. *The goal must be to assess the child's language or languages without standardizing performance, allowing children to demonstrate what they can do in their unique way.* "Assessment must be accompanied by a strong professional development component that focuses on the use of narrative reporting, observation of language development, and sampling the child's language abilities" (pp. 7–8).

4. *A fully contextualized account of the child's language skills requires the involvement of parents and family members, the students themselves, teachers, and staff in providing a detailed picture of the context of language learning and the resources that are available to the child.* "Assessment of the child needs to take into account the entire context in which the child is learning and developing" (p. 8).

Using these guidelines, McLaughlin et al. (1995) recommend what they call *instructionally embedded assessment.* This type of assessment is congruent with the guidelines mentioned concerning appropriate assessment in preschool education as it is "intrinsically linked to program goals and affects instructional practice"; in other words, "the teacher is constantly observing what her children can and cannot do at different times and in different contexts and adjusting her instruction accordingly" (p. 9).

In order to carry out this assessment procedure, teachers follow a six-step process:

1. They make a plan about what, when, and how to assess a child, keeping in mind the need to observe all children, even the ones who are very quiet, to see what they understand.
2. They collect information from a variety of sources, including observations, prompted responses, classroom products, and conversations with family members.
3. They develop a portfolio for the child, which could include observational notes, results of prompted responses, such as audiotapes or dictations, and notes of formal or informal conversations with family members, being careful to collect information about both of the child's languages.
4. They write narrative summaries periodically to combine the material in the portfolio into a form that can be used in conferencing with staff and parents.
5. They meet with family and staff to present information from the portfolios and narrative summaries and to plan instructional strategies.
6. They use the information they have accumulated to inform curriculum development related to a particular child's level and needs.

By combining these assessment steps with knowledge about the developmental pathway that young children take in a second-language acquisition situation and understanding the individual differences that have been discussed, teachers can chart how a child is progressing in acquiring a second language. Keeping in mind that second-language learners' abilities are extremely volatile (see Chapter 4), teachers will need to be constantly evaluating not only what the child is doing but also the circumstances surrounding the child at that time.

Using Assessment Information

The information that can be collected and summarized for each child utilizing the recommended assessment methods can be used in at least four ways: 1) to inform curriculum, 2) to inform parents, 3) to inform other educators who will be working with the child, and 4) to inform decisions about referring the child for further evaluation.

Informing Curriculum   There are many ways that individual assessment of children can inform the curriculum in the classroom. Knowing where a child is in his or her developmental pathway of second-language acquisition means that a teacher can fine tune any of the techniques suggested in Chapters 6 and 7 to fit a particular child's needs. McLaughlin et al. (1995) present the following narratives developed during the assessment process as examples of how assessment can help teachers make curriculum decisions:

Kim Loo

Narrative summary.   After eight months of exposure to English, three-year old Kim is usually silent when she interacts with other children and adults. She is eager to participate in group activities but uses nonverbal means almost entirely . . . Her comprehension of English is improving. She follows directions well and understands short statements and commands in English. According to her parents, Kim speaks and understands her home language, Taiwanese, as would be expected of a child her age.

Instructional strategy.   The teacher decided to use the daily routines of the program to strengthen Kim's English. Because of the repetitive and concrete nature of many everyday routines, they are ideal for helping children acquire vocabulary and word patterns. The staff labeled activities for Kim by talking to her and giving her the words for the activities: "It's snack time. We are having our snacks now. Ready for your snack, Kim?" The teacher also tries to involve Kim in choral activities with other children, such as reciting poems and rhymes. To develop her Taiwanese, the teacher has a Taiwanese-speaking aide read to Kim and other children whose home language is Taiwanese.

Tony Martinez

Narrative summary.   Tony is quite advanced in his English for a four-year old child. He still has some problems finding the right word and his pronunciation is still developing, but he speaks English fluently and loves to participate in activities with English-speaking children. He uses Spanish at home and his parents say that his Spanish is also developing well.

Instructional strategy.   The staff decides to encourage Tony to be involved in dramatic play to increase his English vocabulary. Tony rarely chooses dramatic play. The teacher knows Tony's father is a carpenter and Tony loves woodworking activities. The staff sets up a dramatic play area with tools and carpentry props. To assist in Tony's Spanish language development, the teacher also gives Tony's older sister, who is quite fluent in Spanish, some Spanish books to read with him at home. (p. 18)

By using these types of assessment methods and by charting an individual child's progress, teachers can avoid the one-size-fits-all fallacy of curriculum planning and can modify aspects of the curriculum intentionally to help specific children make developmental gains.

Informing Parents   As discussed in Chapter 8, parents will have many questions about how their child is doing in the classroom. By using observational and narrative techniques, teachers will have actual examples of activities and accomplishments to discuss with parents, helping them to really *see* what is going on in the classroom with their child. Furthermore, teachers will also be able to give parents specific ideas about how the curriculum will be shaped in relation to their child and may even suggest ways that they could work with their child at home.

Informing Other Educators   The transition from preschool to elementary school is a particularly important time for young second-language learners. The program placement that is made will have a major impact on the rest of a child's school experience. Preschool teachers who have developed extensive information about a child's development will be in a position to convey that information to the next group of educators who will be working with the child. Recommendations concerning a particular child will carry much more weight if they are the result of systematic, periodic, and organized assessment than if they are general and vague reports developed only once near the end of the child's preschool experience. Developing methods for making sure that this important information about each child is made available to other educators should be an important part of the assessment process.

Informing Decisions About Referral   When a young second-language–learning child is having problems adjusting to the preschool classroom, teachers will need detailed information to help them make decisions about whether a child might be a candidate for referral to receive other services. Sorting out which behaviors are typical for a young second-language learner and which would be considered a cause for concern should be part of the ongoing assessment process. As the following case study illustrates, careful observation, conferencing with parents, seeking the help of other professionals, and making a plan for modification of the classroom environment can all be part of this process.

TARO: A CASE STUDY

The case of Taro, a Japanese boy who joined the English-language nursery school in September at the age of 2 years 9 months, shows how these assessment elements—observation, conferencing, consultation, and modification—came into play concerning one child's development. Because Taro was only one of the second-language learners in the classroom, because I was not in the classroom every day, and because I was not his teacher, the following observations are not as complete a record of Taro's activities as they might be. Even these observations, however, written each day after visiting the classroom, show how an observational record can help to reveal one child's consistent patterns of behavior and how this information helped teachers make decisions about how they might work effectively with Taro. (Observational notes are in bold; observer's comments are in italics.)

September 19

Taro came in with his mother. He was very tentative and whimpered when he was greeted by Marion. His mother stayed for a good part of the morning, and he stayed in her vicinity but was not tied to her. Just before circle time, Marion asked if his mother was going to leave then. Marion promised that she would hold Taro if he were upset and that his mother could call and check on him. Taro's mother explained all of this to him in

Japanese and then handed him over to Marion and left. Taro did cry loudly for several minutes; then when he was not sobbing, Marion brought him to circle, still keeping him on her lap. During outside time, he separated from her and remained relatively independent for the rest of the morning. After returning to the classroom, he began to play an escape game and doors were closed to contain him. It was very difficult to get him into the routines of eating, cleaning up, brushing teeth, etc. His father came earlier than any other parent for pickup and left quickly.

September 28

... Taro's mother came over to say good-bye to him. He immediately left the water table (where he had been playing alongside Naoshi) and climbed into Marion's lap, even before his mother had left the room ...

Taro seems to have all sorts of problems. Marion is trying to separate which problems might be due to language and which might be developmental.

October 3

Taro clings to the teachers or runs away. He demands their full attention and screams and cries if he does not get it. Marion and Joanne have a conference scheduled with his parents. Marion is concerned that a conference may be difficult for the parents, but she really wants them to know what is going on.

October 12

... Taro arrived with his father. Marion greeted them with "Good morning." Taro's dad said something to him in Japanese which included "morning" and Taro said, "Morning" to Marion, still clinging to his father's leg.

Taro is, indeed, doing better. But he still has a long way to go to become a model member of the class. He still "jitterbugs" around, cannot or will not sit down for circle, and has wild bursts of needing to be held but is unable to derive any comfort from it. Interestingly, there is no question in my mind that Taro's primary problems are not related to language needs, but are social/cognitive problems. A good countercase to thinking that all adjustment must depend on language facility.

At circle time, both Taro and Ling Ling left the circle and wandered around the room. Eventually Marion brought Ling Ling in to sit on her lap. Taro remained on the fringes.

This behavior of Ling Ling and Taro is very unsocial, the most direct repudiation possible of the process of becoming a member of the group.

October 17

At circle time my main focus of observation was Taro because, for the first time that I have seen, Taro was a member of the circle for the whole time today. To begin with, when circle time was announced, Naoshi went to get Taro and brought him into the circle and held his hand, placing himself between Taro and Supat. When the first record was played, however, Taro left the area next to Naoshi and came to stand near the record player as all the other children (including Ling Ling) participated in doing the movements for the record. When everyone sat down after the record, Taro left the corner and went to Marion (who had recently joined the circle). After climbing into her lap briefly, however, he got off and lay down on the floor near her outside the circle holding a toy car.

Naoshi's interest in helping Taro join the circle is interesting. I wonder how he perceives the situation. Does he see it as a big brother–little brother relationship? Naoshi has been a confident member of the classroom almost from the beginning. Will his influence help Taro to become included in the social milieu?

For the rest of the circle Taro migrated back and forth between Marion and Joanne . . . The only time he displayed his shrieking behavior was when Marion left the circle for snack.

Throughout the proceedings Taro never participated in any of the activities, but the fact that he was near the circle was a change from his previous behavior.

October 19

Just as cleanup time was getting underway, I went into the block area and found Naoshi and Taro waltzing around and around with Naoshi holding onto Taro's hand. Taro was giggling and laughing as Naoshi pulled him around. When Naoshi stopped, Taro went out of the area for a minute, then he returned quickly, coming in shrieking in anticipation. Naoshi obliged him by spinning him around again.

Naoshi is definitely working on helping Taro. Marion and I later speculated whether or not Naoshi had been asked by either set of parents to try to help out or if he was undertaking this task on his own.

October 24

During what should have been outside time, the class went to watch a movie in another room because of the rain. It was obvious that Taro was not going to make it through the movie, so I brought him back to the classroom. I got out the plastic pegs and shapes—an activity that he had shown an interest in previously—and for what was probably close to 20 minutes he worked with piling shapes, dumping them over, and piling them again. At one point he was working on circles and was able to pick them out from among the other shapes. I did a lot of naming of colors and shapes, but the only one that got repeated was "yellow one." Otherwise Taro did quite a bit of vocalizing that I couldn't understand.

This session with Taro represented the longest time I have seen him involved in any one activity. He was not as jittery as usual while he was working on this project, and he did not get distracted by anything else— perhaps because there were no other children in the classroom. I noticed that his hand–eye coordination is not good—he often missed the hole in the plastic pieces. He does not seem to have much digital dexterity either. A child with many problems it would seem. But each time I see him he seems to be doing better in the classroom.

At circle time I spent a lot of time getting Taro into the songs. He was at least passively willing and stood in circle first holding Naoshi's hand on one side and mine on the other, then letting me help him do the motions for the first set of songs. After that he broke away, however, and went to lie on the bench.

Taro is more involved in circle time than he has been before.

October 31

Taro is sitting next to me at the circle table using the plastic shapes and the five pegs. I count as he and I take turns putting the shapes on. When he is finished, he turns them over, then starts again. At one point he picked up the pegs and started away from the table. I said, "Taro, show it to Marion" gesturing toward where Marion was painting children's faces (for Halloween) nearby. He did, and she remarked enthusiastically at what a good job he had done.

November 2

A long sequence developed in, around, and above the house area. It started with Byong-sun inside the house by himself looking out the window at the end near the bench where Taro happened to be. When Taro spotted Byong-sun in the window he started to giggle. Then they both giggled and laughed at each other.

When Taro stuck his head in the window, Byong-sun saw him and came back to the window, sticking his hand through again and giggling. Once inside the house, Leandro came to the end of the house with the window and stuck his head out. Taro, who was still on the bench, laughed at Leandro and then stuck his head in the window.

Taro and Byong-sun have had a few giggly interactions before, but this is by far the most extensive interaction between them.

At circle time, I again tried to keep Taro in the circle. He stayed for quite awhile—much of the time lying under my legs. Eventually he got up and left.

Taro seems to be making a lot of progress. Marion and I conferred several times during the day, and we both expressed the opinion that things were going much better. Taro is beginning to make contact with the other children, he is not running away, and he is at least passively a member of circle.

November 7

Today an observer from the local preschool intervention program was in class to observe Taro . . . At one point during the morning, Taro came to the playdough table and sat down next to Ling Ling. I got him some playdough and showed him how the plastic coffee lid could be used to make a circle on the playdough. I also used one of the playdough toys to make a smaller circle. (All of this was being watched by the observer from the early intervention unit.) After this Taro mostly sat flapping the

coffee can top with his fingers close to his face, not attending to the playdough.

In some ways, Taro's behavior was a step forward. He sat down at the table on his own and attended for a while to what I was doing with him. But the flapping of the coffee can lid, as Marion told me later, was interpreted by the early intervention observer as "self-stimulation." Her feeling was that he was a candidate for referral and that he was operating more like a 2-year-old than the 3-year-old he is about to become.

As they were leaving the bench area, Andrew, Supat, and Jessica all stopped at the circle table where they found Taro. The three of them surrounded him and began going "Ah! Ah!" at him from all sides, calling his name, and putting their faces close to his. This developed into a chase game with the three of them chasing Taro into the cubbie area and back into the room.

This behavior by Jessica, Andrew, and Supat is very interesting. I think the initial sequence—calling his name, saying "Ah!," and putting their faces near his—is some kind of mimic of how adults talk to babies. The chase game that followed was very exuberant, and Taro was a very willing participant.

November 16

As I moved over to the circle table, I found Taro on the bench with Byong-sun standing in front of him. Byong-sun was touching Taro's face very gently and smiling at him. While this was going on, Andrew came over and put his face near Taro's and said, "boo, boo," quietly. Then Andrew kissed Taro in the cheek and went away.

Here Byong-sun and Andrew are both treating Taro like a baby. Taro seems to enjoy this kind of attention, but the sequences never last very long.

Having spotted Taro alone in the cubbie area, I decided to see if he would work with me on the pegs and plastic shapes for awhile. I went in to the cubby area and brought him into the classroom to the circle table. I got out the pegs and plastic shapes and he sat right down and started picking out shapes. He picked up a circle. I said, "What's that? That's a circle. Circle?" And he repeated, "Circle?" Then as he continued to pick out shapes, he would ask me "circle?" each time and I would confirm except once when he asked "circle?" and I said, "No,

diamond." He repeated, "Diamond." At another point I said, "Here's a blue one" and he repeated, "Blue one."

*This activity seems to be one of the few activities that Taro can sustain interest in. Is it because it is one of the few that he has been explicitly taught how to do? Perhaps he needs this kind of careful scaffolding to get into **any** activity. Are there children who have to be taught how to play?*

As Taro continued to work with the plastic shapes, Ling Ling came over and sat on the other side of Taro. Because he had recently dumped all the pieces off the pegs, there were some plastic shapes on the table in front of Ling Ling. Taro reached toward the box that still contained most of the shapes, but he did not take any more out. Ling Ling, seeing this, reached across Taro and brought the whole box over to her side. Joanne passed by and Ling Ling said to her, "(unintelligible) Taro." To which Joanne replied, "You're playing with Taro!" After this Taro left the table.

Taro did not object to Ling Ling's incursion on his project, but neither was he able to develop a coordinated effort with the pegs and shapes.

Having left the circle table, Taro went over to the water table, which was filled with straw and farm animals. Andrew saw him there and also came over, saying, "Taro" in a high tone. Andrew started to play with the animals, but Taro did not stay.

When Taro left the water table, he went back over to the circle table where Ling Ling had finished piling the pegs with shapes and then had left. Taro picked up the peg array and dumped it over, spilling some of the shapes on the floor. Seeing what he had done, Taro bent down to pick up several shapes and returned them to the table top. Then he sat down and started to work on the pegs again.

I was very impressed with this sequence on Taro's part. First, because he went back to the activity without any urging from an adult. Second, because he pursued the dropped pieces and retrieved them successfully. And third, because he could organize himself to get back to work on the shapes, again without any adult supervision.

At cleanup time Taro helped me put away the peg array and plastic pieces. He did very well getting the pieces in the box, but then he had trouble with the box top, placing it squarely

180 degrees off where he needed it. I turned it around for him, and he placed the box and the array where they belonged on the shelf.

After this observation, I began to concentrate on taking notes on other second-language–learning children each time I visited the classroom, so I did not collect further detailed descriptions of Taro's activities.

However, several events occurred that were important for Taro. First, in consultation with the preschool early intervention observer, a decision was made to recommend home visits with Taro and his parents around language and play issues. Second, a decision was made to keep Taro in the classroom for the remainder of the year, given the fact that he had made an adjustment and that any other placement would clearly have disrupted him again. After this decision, Marion brought a variety of play items into the classroom for Taro that were more appropriate to a toddler than those already in the classroom. Furthermore, the teachers developed a variety of plans for individualizing aspects of the classroom to promote Taro's development.

CONCLUSION

Clearly one of the reasons that assessing young second-language learners is so difficult is because the use of language is such an integral part of the assessment process. Informal assessment, in particular, is based on being able to converse with children as they are involved in an activity. Children who cannot understand the questions being asked in the assessment situation or do not have sufficient language proficiency to explain what they know are at a disadvantage unless the teacher is aware of these constraints and is prepared to pursue alternative methods of gaining the information.

chapter ten

Developing Effective Preschool Programs for Second-Language Learners

Much of the information in this book is focused on how young children go about learning a second language in a social situation like a preschool classroom and how preschool educators can support that developmental process. But most children who are acquiring a second language are acquiring a second culture as well. In order to plan effective preschool programs for children who are linguistically and culturally diverse, the role of culture in development will need to be taken into consideration as well.

WHAT ABOUT CULTURE?

The basic question, then, is, What is the role of culture in development? Bowman and Stott (1994) write,

> Developmental accomplishments thought to transcend cultural differences include such tasks as establishing mutually satisfying social relationships, organizing and integrating perceptions, learning language, developing category systems, thinking, imagining,

and creating. Since children's growth and development are reasonably orderly, developmental achievements are learned in a similar fashion by all children and occur in predictable sequences. (p. 120)

In other words, all typically developing children, no matter what cultural group they belong to, are expected to engage in behavior meant to master the types of tasks listed by Bowman and Stott (1994). All of these tasks are certainly ones that preschool educators would recognize as important in the early childhood period, and making appropriate developmental progress related to these achievements can be considered the work of early childhood.

This is, however, only part of the developmental picture. Bowman and Stott (1994) continue,

> Developmental milestones, however, take on their *meaning* only in the context of social life. The meaning of behavior is determined by the values and expectations of members of a culture as passed from one generation to the next. Children, therefore, learn to balance their needs and wishes with the constraints and freedoms of the social world in which they live, to express their developmental predispositions in ways that are consistent with their family's and culture's practices. (p. 120)

In other words, even the behaviors that young children share with all other children are expressed and interpreted within a cultural setting. For example, expectations and practices related to such issues as toilet training, discipline, separation, and socialization all take on cultural meaning and cultural interpretations. Families will hold certain attitudes and beliefs about these issues depending on their cultural heritage and their own personal experiences.

How does this play out in relation to how children learn? Bowman and Stott (1994) contend,

> Cultural factors play an important role in determining how and what children learn (Rogoff, Gauvain, & Ellis, 1984). They interface with age/stage potential, personal characteristics, and experience—giving them direction and substance . . . Cultural differences can lead teachers to misunderstand children, to misassess their developmental competence, and to plan incorrectly for their educational achievement. (p. 121)

For these reasons, then, it is clear that preschool educators will need to be responsive to cultural differences as well as linguistic differences in planning curricular and assessment activities. Knowing what cultural differences make a difference for young children and finding out how they are expressed at home and in the preschool setting will be necessary components for effective preschool education programs for children who are linguistically and culturally diverse. As Bowman and Stott (1994) conclude, "Educating all children will require the will and commitment to understand and respond to cultural difference. To the extent that teachers know and understand how children's past experiences have been organized and explained, they are better able to fashion new ones for them" (p. 131).

This concern for the importance of culture in development has sparked considerable discussion about just how appropriate the developmentally appropriate practice standards are that have defined effective practice in early childhood classrooms since the mid-1980s (Mallory & New, 1994). Clearly, if these standards are meant to express a single cultural representation—what might be called a European American representation—then they cannot be appropriate for all children, because many children come to early childhood classrooms from very different cultural backgrounds. For this reason, effective early childhood practice is now defined as being culturally as well as developmentally appropriate (Bredekamp & Rosegrant, 1992, 1995). What this means for early childhood education for children who are linguistically and culturally diverse is the topic of the next section.

RESPONDING TO LINGUISTIC AND CULTURAL DIVERSITY: RECOMMENDATIONS FOR EFFECTIVE EARLY CHILDHOOD EDUCATION

In recognition of the growing number of children from linguistically and culturally diverse families who are attending preschool programs, the National Association for the Education of Young Children (NAEYC) (1996) has issued a position statement "Responding to Linguistic and Cultural Diversity—Recommendations for Effective Early Childhood Education." This position paper makes a strong statement concerning the potential problems related to the loss of a first language, and, in recognition of the variety of cultural representations with which children arrive in the classroom, recommends that early childhood educators develop flexible strategies for working with families from linguistic and culturally diverse backgrounds.

The position statement is divided into four sets of recommendations: recommendations for working with children, for working with families, for professional preparation, and for programs and practice. In the following section, each of the recommendations for developing an effective preschool program for children who are linguistically and culturally diverse is discussed, particularly in reference to the material from this book.[1]

Recommendations for Working with Children

- *Recognize that all children are cognitively, linguistically, and emotionally connected to the language and culture of their home.*

  This recommendation reinforces and extends the important premise that parents are the first educators of their children. As discussed in Chapter 1, children's earliest learning experiences occur in the context of the home language and culture. An effective preschool program will recognize and honor the importance of the cognitive, linguistic, and emotional understandings that a child brings to the preschool setting from home. By collecting cultural information (see Chapter 6), by interviewing parents (see Chapter 6), and by making home visits (see Chapter 8), preschool educators will be able to develop their own understandings about the meaning of the home language and culture in the lives of the children they serve. As children who are linguistically and culturally diverse move from home to preschool, they should never be made to feel that they must choose between the ways of their family and friends and the ways of their school. Instead, they must be assisted in adding to their cultural and linguistic repertoire in this new setting without feeling they must give up their cultural and linguistic heritage.

---

[1]The following recommendations and bulleted entries are from the National Association for the Education of Young Children. (1996, January). NAEYC position statement: Responding to linguistic and cultural diversity—Recommendations for effective early childhood education. *Young Children*, pp. 7–12.

- *Acknowledge that children can demonstrate their knowledge and capabilities in many ways.*
  As discussed in Chapter 9, when children are at a linguistic disadvantage, it will not be possible for them to demonstrate their knowledge through verbal communication for quite some time. Preschool educators, therefore, will need to develop other ways of helping children show what they know, including the use of extensive observations and nonverbal tasks.

  Furthermore, children from different cultural backgrounds may also have different ways of expressing themselves. Teachers will need to be alert to the possibility that a child's behavior, although different from other children's, is, however, an expression of what that child's understandings are at that time and will need to use that as the relevant starting point for that child.
- *Understand that without comprehensible input, second-language learning can be difficult.*
  Comprehensible input refers to the types of modifications of language that educators can use when communicating with second-language learners, such as those discussed in Chapters 6 and 7. Techniques such as buttressed communication,

repetition, running commentary, and context-embedded talk all make it more likely that a second-language–learning child will be able to understand what is being communicated and will begin to get an idea of how the new language works.

In order for these techniques to work, however, preschool educators will need to ensure that second-language learners feel safe and included in the classroom. As discussed in Chapter 2, there is a double bind for children who are in a social situation in which they cannot speak the language: In order to begin to understand and speak the language, they need to be in social contact with those who already speak the language; but in order to get into social contact, they need to be able to speak the language. As discussed in Chapter 6, there are a variety of ways in which teachers can help second-language–learning children feel more comfortable and competent, including providing safe havens where second-language learners can play independently and developing small-group activities that include second-language learners. Involving the English-speaking children in helping the second-language learners can also be a key component of an effective program. Leaving second-language–learning children alone to figure it out by themselves is not an appropriate strategy.

Recommendations for Working with Families

- *Actively involve parents and families in the early learning program and setting.*
  It may be difficult to communicate with families who come from different cultural and linguistic backgrounds, particularly if there are no liaison personnel who speak the home language of the families. However, it should be possible for preschool educators to get information about families, using techniques like the questionnaires suggested in Chapters 6 and 8, so each family's interests can be included in the classroom. Bringing the home language and culture into the classroom will make a child's transition to the new setting more comfortable, will let parents of second-language learners know that the program values their knowledge and interests, and will benefit the English-speaking parents and children in developing multicultural understandings.

- *Encourage and assist all parents in becoming knowledgeable about the cognitive value for children of knowing more than one language, and provide them with strategies to support, maintain, and preserve home-language learning.*
  As outlined in Chapter 8, parents of second-language–learning children often have questions about whether they should be maintaining and developing their home language with their children. Preschool educators can support parents by letting them know how important their role is in their child's development and how important their home language is in accomplishing this.

  However, simply believing that maintaining the home language is a good idea may not be sufficient because children are likely to try to reduce the cognitive load by dropping the home language. This is the point at which preschool educators can play a crucial role, helping parents develop strategies for continuing the use of the home language within the family context, for seeking social situations outside the family where the language is spoken, and for traveling to areas where the home language is the primary language. In order to help parents with these issues, preschool educators will need to be extremely knowledgeable about the messages that parents receive from the media, the traditional educational establishment, and their children. Informing parents in advance about these issues will assist them in developing the strategies needed in order to maintain their home language before language loss begins.

- *Recognize that parents and families rely on caregivers and educators to honor and support their children in the cultural values and norms of the home.*
  Most of the discussion in this book has focused on the process that children who are linguistically and culturally diverse go through to become bilingual and bicultural in a second-language and second-culture setting. This recommendation, however, points out that preschool educators will also need to begin to accommodate their practice in ways that demonstrate that they are developing bilingual and bicultural sensitivities. In order to communicate effectively with parents who are linguistically and culturally diverse, preschool educators will need to let parents know that they understand and

value family norms. Acquiring the necessary knowledge along these lines will take time and persistence (see Chapters 6 and 8 for suggestions), but will certainly pay off in increased understanding and communication. Furthermore, once preschool educators have developed cultural understandings, it will be possible to bring those understandings into the curriculum of the classroom and include them in the assessment process.

Recommendations for Professional Preparation

- *Provide early childhood educators with professional preparation and development in the areas of culture, language, and diversity.*

  Making sense of what children who are linguistically and culturally diverse are experiencing in the classroom requires a theoretical and practical framework that goes beyond the basics of child development. Understanding, facilitating, and assessing second-language acquisition will require specific knowledge on the part of preschool educators, knowledge that traditional coursework may not provide. Furthermore, preschool educators will need to take the time to study and reflect on the cultural differences that may make a difference in young children's behavior and to think about how those differences can influence what goes on in their classrooms.

- *Recruit and support early childhood educators who are trained in languages other than English.*

  Bringing bilingual and bicultural professionals into the classroom with appropriate support can result in a myriad of positive effects. First, by recruiting and supporting early childhood educators who are bilingual and bicultural, a program demonstrates its commitment to broadening its scope and becoming more responsive to the needs of the children it serves. Second, if there are well-developed opportunities for constructive discussions among staff members, conversations can occur that will help all staff members develop an understanding of what it means to come from a different language and/or cultural background. Third, communication with children and parents who share the first language with a bilingual early childhood educator will be facilitated, and home and preschool contacts may be increased and may be more beneficial for both the parents and the program. And fourth, the presence of a bilingual and bicultural early childhood educator sends a powerful message to all children and all parents that more than one language and more than one culture is honored and valued by the program.

Recommendations for Programs and Practice

- *Recognize that children can and will acquire the use of English even when their home language is used and respected.*
  This recommendation actually combines two important points: 1) young children can and will learn a second language in a supportive social setting, and 2) they do not have to give up their first language in order to learn a second language.

  The first part of this recommendation is supported by the information concerning the developmental pathway of home-language use, nonverbal communication, formulaic language use, and productive language use, which research has shown is common for young children in a social setting in which a second language is used (see Chapters 3 and 4). Of course, like all developmental processes, there are differences in how individual children go about this process (see Chapter 5). These differences, based on underlying factors such as motivation, exposure, age, and personality, may affect the cognitive and social strategies that young children bring to the task of second-language acquisition, but it is clear that typically developing young children can successfully acquire a second language in a setting such as a preschool classroom.

  The second part of this recommendation is, however, more problematic and refers to a common belief that in order to successfully learn a second language, the first language must be abandoned. Where does this belief come from and how can it be countered?

  This belief is rooted in a model of language learning that I call the *single-container theory*. In this conceptualization there is limited cognitive capacity available for learning language. This cognitive space can be thought of as analogous to an empty glass. As a child begins to learn a home language, the glass begins to fill up with the first-language liquid. Fortunately, in this view, the glass is just the right size to hold all of

the first-language liquid; once the glass is full, the child has successfully achieved first-language acquisition.

In this model, difficulties arise, however, if part way through this process a second-language liquid is poured into the same glass, with the same capacity, at the same time. In this case, the single-container theory predicts there will be a mixture of the two languages, as the two liquids flow together, resulting in semilingualism (incomplete learning of either language), or there will not be enough room for the second liquid, resulting in an overflow and, therefore, lack of complete second-language acquisition. In either of these cases, the recommended remedy is to empty the glass of the first-language liquid, so that there will be no competing language to confuse the child or keep the child from learning the second language.

The competing model of language learning is what I call the *multiple-container theory*. In this theory, the child's first-language acquisition is again represented by a single glass that is filled with the first-language liquid, just as in the single-container model above. In this model, however, when the child is exposed to a second language, a new glass is added. This new glass comes with some liquid already in it—the child's knowledge of how language works—but it needs to be filled with second-language liquid in order for it to be useful to the child. In this model, the two glasses can continue to be filled simultaneously and can contain different amounts of liquid depending on exposure to and use of the language. Furthermore, the amount of liquid in either glass can fluctuate depending on the amount of language learning that is occurring in either language at a given time. If the child is exposed to a third, fourth, or fifth language, this model provides that a new glass will be started for each with no need to remove any of the previous glasses. If one of the languages is not used, however, the liquid in that glass will eventually dry up and ability in that language will be lost.

These two models represent two types of bilingualism called *subtractive* and *additive*. Educators may give parents entirely opposite advice depending on which of these models of second-language learning they support. Educators who believe that a first language interferes with the learning of a second language, the single-container theory, often recommend to parents that they abandon the home language and make every effort to remove their children from contact with the first language. This policy results in subtractive bilingualism, the replacement of the first language with the second. As discussed in Chapter 8, research has shown that this model is not accurate, and that the results of such policies have been detrimental to both children and families.

Educators who believe that well-developed first-language acquisition enhances the learning of a second language, the multiple-container theory, recommend that the home language be maintained and offer parents important advice related to strategies that they will need to use in order to support development in the first language. This policy results in additive bilingualism, when the second language is added to the first language. As discussed in Chapter 8, research has demonstrated that there are a variety of cognitive, emotional, and cultural benefits to first-language maintenance as children learn a second language.

This recommendation, then, refers to the second of these models, the one that supports additive bilingualism. In order for this recommendation to become accepted, educators who understand the importance of additive bilingualism will need to be prepared to help explain the multiple-container model to other educators and to parents.

- *Support and preserve home-language usage.*
  Given the negative consequences of subtractive bilingualism, the need to help parents continue the use of the first language at home with their children becomes obvious. This recommendation requires that effective programs for children who are linguistically and culturally diverse take an active stance in informing, strategizing, and supporting parents' efforts to keep the home language alive for their children (see Chapter 8).

- *Develop and provide alternative and creative strategies for young children's learning.*
  Having children who are linguistically and culturally diverse in the classroom means that preschool educators must always take into consideration how each learning activity will need to be set up in order for optimum learning to occur. By providing a multitude of ways and modes that children can use to arrive at new understandings of a topic, preschool educators will make it possible for all children to participate more fully in the construction of their own knowledge.

TEACHER PREPARATION AND STAFF DEVELOPMENT

Although only two of the previous recommendations have been placed under the category of professional preparation, it is obvious that both preservice and in-service programs for preschool educators will need to reexamine the premises from which they operate and reorient the way they prepare preschool educators if the NAEYC recommendations are to be put into effect. Some suggestions for the types of changes that will be necessary include the following:

1. Preschool educators will need to develop new understandings about the role of language and culture in development and the pathways that children take in becoming bilingual and bicultural.
2. Preschool educators will need to realize that developmentally appropriate practice must be interpreted to include development as expressed in other cultural groups.

3. Preschool educators will need to be prepared to examine their own cultural and linguistic heritage so they can begin to gain an understanding of the cultural lens that they bring to the classroom and to examine their attitudes about other linguistic and cultural groups.
4. Preschool educators will need to reflect on the ways that these understandings can and will affect their practice.
5. Preschool educators will need to be well versed in the research related to second-language acquisition so they can help parents develop strategies for home language preservation.
6. Preschool educators will need to learn how to observe and assess children during ongoing activities in the classroom (see Chapter 9), looking for alternative and nontraditional ways that children express their understandings.

Will all of these changes be easily or quickly accomplished? Of course not. Are they necessary? Absolutely. Given the statistics cited in Chapter 1 concerning the numbers of children from linguistically and culturally diverse backgrounds who are entering preschools, it is clear that business as usual is no longer possible. Responding appropriately to children who are culturally and linguistically diverse and their families will require new information, new attitudes, and new practices on the part of preschool educators. The information provided in this book will help preschool educators begin the process of developing these new understandings.

References

Beals, D., & Snow, C. (1994). "Thunder is when the angels are upstairs bowling": Narratives and explanations at the dinner table. *Journal of Narrative and Life History, 4*(4), 331–352.

Bowman, B., & Stott, F. (1994). Understanding development in a cultural context: The challenge for teachers. In B. Mallory & R. New (Eds.), *Diversity and developmentally appropriate practices: Challenges for early childhood education* (pp. 119–133). New York: Teachers College Press.

Bredekamp, S. (1987). *Developmentally appropriate practice in early childhood programs serving children from birth through age 8* (Rev. ed.). Washington, DC: National Association for the Education of Young Children.

Bredekamp, S., & Rosegrant, T. (1992). Reaching potentials: Introduction. In S. Bredekamp & T. Rosegrant (Eds.), *Reaching potentials: Vol. 1. Appropriate curriculum and assessment* (pp. 2–8). Washington, DC: National Association for the Education of Young Children.

Bredekamp, S., & Rosegrant, T. (Eds.). (1995). *Reaching potentials: Vol. 2. Transforming early childhood curriculum and assessment.* Washington, DC: National Association for the Education of Young Children.

Bunce, B.H. (1995). *Building a language-focused curriculum for the preschool classroom: Vol. II. A planning guide.* Baltimore: Paul H. Brookes Publishing Co.

Bunce, B.H., & Watkins, R.V. (1995). Language intervention in a preschool classroom: Implementing a language-focused curriculum. In M.L. Rice & K.A. Wilcox (Eds.), *Building a language-focused curriculum for the preschool classroom: Vol. 1. A foundation for lifelong communication* (pp. 39–71). Baltimore: Paul H. Brookes Publishing Co.

Chittenden, E., & Courtney, R. (1989). Assessment of young children's reading: Documentation as an alternative to testing. In D. Strickland & L. Morrow (Eds.), *Emerging literacy: Young children learn to read and write* (pp. 107–120). Newark, NJ: International Reading Association.

Christian, D., & Whitcher, A. (1995). *Directory of two-way bilingual programs in the United States.* Washington, DC: National Center for Research in Cultural Diversity and Second Language Learning, Center for Applied Linguistics.

Collier, V. (1987, December). Age and rate of acquisition of second language for academic purposes. *TESOL Quarterly, 21*(4), 617–641.

Collier, V. (1989, September). How long? A synthesis of research on academic achievement in second language. *TESOL Quarterly, 23*(3), 509–531.

Cummins, J. (1984). *Bilingualism and special education: Issues in assessment and pedagogy.* San Diego: College-Hill Press.

Engel, B. (1990). An approach to evaluation in reading and writing. In C. Kamii (Ed.), *Achievement testing in early childhood education: Games grownups play* (pp. 119–134). Washington, DC: National Association for the Education of Young Children.

Ervin-Tripp, S. (1974, June). Is second language learning like the first? *TESOL Quarterly, 8*(2), 111–127.

Fantini, A. (1985). *Language acquisition of a bilingual child.* San Diego: College-Hill Press.

Garnica, O. (1983). Social dominance and conversational interaction— The omega child in the classroom. In C. Wallat & J. Green (Eds.), *Ethnography and language in educational settings* (pp. 229–252). Norwood, NJ: Ablex Publishing.

Garvey, C. (1977). *Play.* Cambridge, MA: Harvard University Press.

Genishi, C., & Brainard, M. (1995). Assessment of bilingual children: A dilemma seeking solutions. In E. Garcia & B. McLaughlin (Eds.), *Meeting the challenge of linguistic and cultural diversity in early childhood education* (pp. 49–63). New York: Teachers College Press.

Genishi, C., Dyson, A., & Fassler, R. (1994). Language and diversity in early childhood: Whose voices are appropriate? In B. Mallory & R. New (Eds.), *Diversity and developmentally appropriate practices: Challenges for early childhood education* (pp. 250–268). New York: Teachers College Press.

Goodman, K., Goodman, Y., & Hood, W. (1989). *The whole language evaluation book.* Portsmouth, NH: Heinemann.

Goodwin, W.L., & Goodwin, L.D. (1982). Measuring young children. In B. Spodek (Ed.), *Handbook of research in early childhood education* (pp. 523–563). New York: Free Press.

Hakuta, K. (1978). A report on the development of grammatical morphemes in a Japanese girl learning English as a second language. In E. Hatch (Ed.), *Second language acquisition: A book of readings* (pp. 132–147). Rowley, MA: Newbury House Publishers.

Hakuta, K. (1986). *Mirror of language: The debate on bilingualism.* New York: Basic Books.

Headden. S. (1995, September 25). One nation, one language? *U.S. News & World Report, 119*(12), 38–42.

Hill, E. (1980). *Where's Spot?* New York: G.P. Putnam's Sons.

Hirschler, J. (1991). *Preschool children's help to second language learners.* Unpublished doctoral dissertation, Harvard Graduate School of Education, Cambridge, MA.

Hirschler, J. (1994, Winter). Preschool children's help to second language learners. *Journal of Educational Issues of Language Minority Students, 14,* 227–240.

Hornblower, M. (1995, October 9). Putting tongues in check. *Time,* 40–50.

Huang, J., & Hatch, E. (1978). A Chinese child's acquisition of English. In E. Hatch (Ed.), *Second language acquisition: A book of readings* (pp. 118–131). Rowley, MA: Newbury House Publishers.

Itoh, H., & Hatch, E. (1978). Second language acquisition: A case study. In E. Hatch (Ed.), *Second language acquisition: A book of readings* (pp. 76–88). Rowley, MA: Newbury House Publishers.

Kagan, S., & Garcia, E. (1991). Education of culturally and linguistically diverse preschoolers: Moving the agenda. *Early Childhood Research Quarterly, 6,* 427–443.

Krashen, S. (1980). The input hypothesis. In J. Alatis (Ed.), *Current issues in bilingual education* (pp. 168–180). Washington, DC: Georgetown University Press.

Mallory, B., & New, R. (Eds.). (1994). *Diversity and developmentally appropriate practices: Challenges for early childhood education.* New York: Teachers College Press.

McLaughlin, B., Blanchard, A., & Osanai, Y. (1995). *Assessing language development in bilingual preschool children.* Washington, DC: George Washington University. (The National Clearinghouse for Bilingual Education, #22, June)

Meisel, J. (1989). Early differentiation of languages in bilingual children. In K. Hylterstam & L. Obler (Eds.), *Bilingualism across the lifespan: Aspects of acquisition, maturity, and loss* (pp. 13–54). Cambridge, England: Cambridge University Press.

Meisels, S. (1994). Designing meaningful measurements for early childhood. In B. Mallory & R. New (Eds.), *Diversity and developmentally appropriate practices: Challenges for early childhood education* (pp. 202–222). New York: Teachers College Press.

Meyer, C. (1989). *The role of peer relationships in the socialization of children to preschool: A Korean example.* Unpublished doctoral dissertation, Ohio State University, Columbus.

National Association for the Education of Young Children. (1996, January). NAEYC position statement: Responding to linguistic and cultural diversity—Recommendations for effective early childhood education. *Young Children,* 4–12.

Rice, M.L. (1991). Children with specific language impairment: Toward a model of teachability. In N. Krasnegor, D. Rumbaugh, R. Schiefelbusch, & M. Studdert-Kennedy (Eds.), *Biological and behavioral determinants of language development* (pp. 447–480). Hillsdale, NJ: Lawrence Erlbaum Associates.

Rice, M.L., & Wilcox, K.A. (1990). *Language Acquisition Preschool: A model preschool for language disordered and ESL children.* (Grant No. G008630279). Washington, DC: U.S. Department of Education, Office of Special Education Programs.

Rice, M.L., & Wilcox, K.A. (Eds.). (1995). *Building a language-focused curriculum for the preschool classroom: Vol. 1. A foundation for lifelong communication.* Baltimore: Paul H. Brookes Publishing Co.

Rodriguez, R. (1983). *Hunger of memory: The education of Richard Rodriguez.* New York: Bantam Books.

Rogoff, B., Gauvain, M., & Ellis, S. (1984). Development viewed in its cultural context. In M. Bornstein & M. Lamb (Eds.), *Developmental psychology* (pp. 533–571). Hillsdale, NJ: Lawrence Erlbaum Associates.

Saunders, G. (1988). *Bilingual children: From birth to teens.* Philadelphia: Multilingual Matters.

Saville-Troike, M. (1987). Dilingual discourse: The negotiation of meaning without a common code. *Linguistics, 25,* 81–106.

Saville-Troike, M. (1988). Private speech: Evidence for second language learning strategies during the "silent period." *Journal of Child Language, 15,* 567–590.

Shatz, M., & Gelman, R. (1977). Beyond syntax: The influence of conversational constraints on speech modifications. In C. Snow & C. Ferguson (Eds.), *Talking to children: Language input and acquisition* (pp. 189–198). New York: Cambridge University Press.

Smith, M. (1996). *Teacher–child interaction in early childhood education classrooms: Theoretical and practical perspectives.* Unpublished doctoral dissertation, Clark University, Worcester, MA.

Smith, H., & Heckman, P. (1995). The Mexican-American war. In E. Garcia & B. McLaughlin (Eds.), *Meeting the challenge of linguistic and cultural diversity in early childhood education* (pp. 64–84). New York: Teachers College Press.

Snow, C. (1983). Age differences in second language acquisition: Research findings and folk psychology. In K. Bailey, M. Long, & S. Peck (Eds.), *Second language acquisition studies.* (pp. 141–150). Rowley, MA: Newbury House.

Snow, C., & Hoefnagel-Hohle, M. (1977). Age differences in the pronunciation of foreign sounds. *Language and Speech, 20,* 357-365.

SocioTechnical Research Applications, Inc. (1996). *Report on the ACYF bilingual/multicultural survey.* Washington, DC: The Head Start Bureau.

Sutherland, Z., & Arbuthnot, M. (1991). *Children and books* (8th ed.). New York: HarperCollins.

Tabors, P. (1982). *Panos: A case study of a bilingual child.* Unpublished manuscript, Harvard Graduate School of Education, Cambridge, MA.

Tabors, P. (1984). *The identification of categories of environmental support available for second language acquisition in a nursery school classroom.*

Unpublished qualifying paper, Harvard Graduate School of Education, Cambridge, MA.

Tabors, P. (1987). *The development of communicative competence by second language learners in a nursery school classroom: An ethnolinguistic study.* Unpublished doctoral dissertation, Harvard Graduate School of Education, Cambridge, MA.

Tabors, P. (1988). *The plan for the Demonstration School.* Unpublished manuscript, University of Lowell, Lowell, MA.

Tabors, P., & Snow, C. (1994). English as a second language in pre-schools. In F. Genesee (Ed.), *Educating second language children: The whole child, the whole curriculum, the whole community* (pp. 103–125). New York: Cambridge University Press.

Taeschner, T. (1983). *The sun is feminine: A study of language acquisition in bilingual children.* New York: Springer-Verlag.

Teale, W. (1988). Developmentally appropriate assessment of reading and writing in the early childhood classroom. *The Elementary School Journal, 89*(2), 173–184.

Williams, L.R., & De Gaetano, Y. (1985). *ALERTA: A multicultural, bilingual approach to teaching young children.* Menlo Park, CA: Addison-Wesley.

Wong Fillmore, L. (1976). *The second time around: Cognitive and social strategies in second language acquisition.* Unpublished doctoral dissertation, Stanford University, Palo Alto, CA.

Wong Fillmore, L. (1979). Individual differences in second language acquisition. In C.J. Fillmore, D. Kempler, & W. S-Y. Wang (Eds.), *Individual differences in language ability and language behavior* (pp. 203–228) New York: Academic Press.

Wong Fillmore, L. (1991a). Language and cultural issues in the early education of language minority children. In S. Kagan (Ed.), *The care and education of America's young children: Obstacles and opportunities. Ninetieth yearbook of the National Society for the Study of Education, Part I* (pp. 30–49). Chicago: University of Chicago Press.

Wong Fillmore, L. (1991b). When learning a second language means losing the first. *Early Childhood Research Quarterly , 6*(3), 323–346.

Yim, M.K. (1984). *Turn the page please: Learning a second language through picture book reading.* Unpublished qualifying paper, Harvard Graduate School of Education, Cambridge, MA.

Index

Page numbers followed by *t* or *f* indicate tables or figures, respectively.